Praise from readers and health professionals for

LINDA SPANGLE and *Life Is Hard,*
Food Is Easy: The 5-Step Plan to Overcome
Emotional Eating and Lose Weight on Any Diet

Linda's book addresses the emotional aspects of eating and weight loss extremely well. It goes hand-in-hand with the Curves for Women Program, "Permanent Results without Permanent Dieting." Linda gives some very realistic and concrete suggestions for figuring out what's really going on when we overeat. —KIM HUSS, CURVES FOR WOMEN OWNER

As a dietitian and weight-loss counselor, I have been able to apply and use many of Linda's concepts and methods in my sessions with clients. I believe that one must dig deep and uncover what truly lies beneath the problem, not just find a solution to what seems apparent on the outside. —VANESSA ALDAZ, MPH, RD

Unlike many books on emotional eating, Linda's book gives readers everyday tools to overcome their challenges with weight loss. We recommend it to all of our clients at the Denver Metabolic Research Weight-Loss Center. —DAPHNE RICHARDS, WEIGHT-LOSS COUNSELOR

I couldn't put this book down. The author seemed to be talking to me! I have read many diet books in the past, but this book describes the true reason behind overeating. She walks you through why you must deal with the problems within before you can be successful on any diet program. —KJ

This book isn't another fad diet—it focuses on *why* we reach for food, no matter what we weigh. The author will make you think. She has practical suggestions for breaking through our emotional barriers and taking care of ourselves instead of eating. —SUSAN

100 DAYS *of* WEIGHT LOSS

ALSO BY LINDA SPANGLE

Life Is Hard, Food Is Easy

Success in a Shaker Jar

100 DAYS *of*
WEIGHT
LOSS

The Secret to Being
Successful on
Any Diet Plan

A DAILY MOTIVATOR

LINDA SPANGLE, RN, MA

THOMAS NELSON
Since 1798

NASHVILLE   DALLAS   MEXICO CITY   RIO DE JANEIRO   BEIJING

© by Linda Spangle, 2006, 2007.

Published in Nashville, Tennessee, by Thomas Nelson.
Thomas Nelson is a registered trademark of Thomas Nelson, Inc.

Thomas Nelson, Inc. titles may be purchased in bulk for educational,
business, fund-raising, or sales promotional use. For information,
please e-mail SpecialMarkets@ThomasNelson.com.

Library of Congress Cataloging-in-Publication Data
Spangle, Linda.
100 days of weight loss : the secret to being successful on any diet
plan / Linda Spangle.
p. cm.
"A daily motivator."
Originally published: Denver, Colo. : SunQuest Media, © 2006.
Includes bibliographical references and index.
ISBN: 978-1-4016-0373-1
1. Reducing diets. 2. Weight loss. I. Title. II. Title: One hundred
days of weight loss.
RM222.2.S674 2007
613.2'5—dc22

2007021042

Printed in the United States of America

13 QG 9 8 7 6 5

❧ CONTENTS ❧

CONTENTS

CONTENTS

DAYS 51-60 EMOTIONAL EATING

DAYS 61-70 TRIGGERS AND WORD PLAY

DAYS 71-80 GROWING STRONGER

CONTENTS

❧ WELCOME! ❧

I think I know why you're here. Somehow you want to be able to change your future. I'm guessing that you'd love to get control over food, lose a bunch of extra pounds, and then maintain your weight for the rest of your life.

Well, you've come to the right place. During the next 100 days, you can achieve phenomenal progress toward reaching these goals. But the amazing part is, you will feel like it was *easy*. Here's how it works.

Each day you will complete one mini-lesson related to some aspect of managing your weight. Then with time, you'll learn how to slip these tools into your daily routines. Eventually, just like putting on your shoes or brushing your teeth, your new skills will become second nature. And when they do, you'll have found the secret to long-term success!

Why it works

In my 20 years of working with overweight individuals, I've found that one problem shows up again and again. In spite of their initial enthusiasm, most people average just three to four weeks on a diet before they fall off the wagon. The reason? Real life gets in the way!

As many dieters do, you probably start out strong. But then you get worn down by life challenges such as family, work, stress, finances, or even emotional struggles. At some point, the need to *feel better* becomes stronger than your desire to lose weight. Before long, you slip off your diet and reach for a piece of chocolate cake or a bag of potato chips.

After you've messed up, you may have a hard time getting

back on your diet. Eventually, you just give up on your goal of losing weight—at least for a while.

Does this sound way too familiar? If so, you may need an entirely new approach for managing your weight. While a healthy diet and exercise plan can certainly help, sometimes it takes more than that. What you really need is an easy set of tools that will help you to calm, nurture, and energize yourself so that food doesn't have to do it for you.

In my book *Life Is Hard, Food Is Easy*, I showed readers how to stop using food as the solution to their emotional needs. Now I've divided these skills into small, bite-sized pieces, so you can easily fit them into your hectic days.

Many of these lessons will simply remind you of things you already know. But others will pull you deeper, helping you cope more effectively with issues such as weak motivation, low self-esteem, and emotional eating. As you complete these one-a-day lessons, you'll build a solid weight-management framework you can stand on forever.

How to do the 100 Days Program

Because this book is designed to work with any diet plan, you get to choose your own method for losing weight. So decide on the program you want to use, and then simply follow these steps to a successful 100 days!

Step One: Choose your best diet plan

Think carefully about what works for you. Do you enjoy going to weight-loss groups, or do you prefer meeting one-on-one with a counselor? Maybe you'll go to a commercial diet program or hire a personal weight-loss coach. Or you might even design your own system using a new diet book, an Internet resource, or a plan that you've followed in the past.

After you've chosen your diet plan, make sure you know your recommended daily calorie levels or the number of servings for each of the food groups. You'll also want to think about how you'll monitor or track your food intake to see whether you've met your diet plan's requirements.

TAKE THE DIET QUIZ

If you need help with choosing a diet plan, take the quiz at www.thedietquiz.com.

Based on the amount of weight you want to lose as well as your age, history, body type, and personal preferences, this quiz helps you pick the diet plan that best matches your needs and gives you the greatest chance for success.

Step Two: Follow your plan for 100 days

Plan to complete one lesson from this book each day, setting a goal of staying on your weight-loss plan for *100 consecutive days*. If for some reason that's not a realistic time frame, you can space the lessons any way you want.

If you take a vacation or slip off your diet for a few days, don't start over at Day 1. Just pick up on the lessons where you left off and continue moving forward. Remember, your goal is to log a total of 100 days, even if it takes you longer than that to accomplish it.

One hundred days is a magical amount of time. Because it forces you to stay focused and consistent, your efforts will last far longer than they might otherwise. Any time you struggle and you're tempted to go off your plan, use the goal of reaching 100 days as a way to strengthen your resolve.

Step Three: Track your progress

Before you begin your 100 days, purchase a special notebook or journal for tracking your progress. With each day's lesson, record your answers to the "Today" assignment as well as any other insights or ideas that will help you in the future.

In addition, come up with a *visual* way to track your 100 days. You might write each day's number on a calendar or on a wall chart. Or maybe you can record them in your daily planner or on a graph you create on your computer. Then watch as the days accumulate, moving you closer toward your goal.

Create a vision for the future

Think for a minute about *why* you want to lose weight. Do you have any immediate goals such as feeling better or wearing certain clothes? Maybe you hope to decrease your back pain or lower your blood pressure. Perhaps you want to set a healthier example for your children.

In your 100 days notebook, write down at least 10 reasons why you want to lose weight and maintain your success. Here are a few ideas to get you started:

- Feel better; have less back and knee pain

- Have more energy; be able to exercise more easily

- Be healthier; lower my blood pressure/cholesterol

- Improve my self-esteem and my confidence

- Wear a bathing suit without embarrassment

Tape copies of this list to your mirror and your refrigerator. Write your list on a small card and carry it with you. Read it daily for at least the first week or two of this program.

Anytime you feel discouraged or tempted to give up, review your list again and remind yourself: "This is why I'm doing the 100 Days Program and I'm absolutely sticking with my plan."

To build your vision of success even stronger, try to picture yourself at a healthy weight. Pull one of your favorite outfits out of your closet, and hang it where you can see it often. Try on a pair of jeans that are too small right now, and then imagine how you'll feel when they fit perfectly.

If you have trouble *seeing* yourself thin, think about how you'll *feel* after you've lost weight. For example, picture yourself moving gracefully through narrow store aisles or fitting comfortably into theater or airplane seats. Use these images to help keep your motivation strong and focused.

Using the scale

Do you have a love-hate relationship with your bathroom scale? In reality, the scale is an important tool in your program. If you pretend that you don't own one or you avoid weighing yourself because you're afraid of what the scale might say, you may need to change the way you approach this area.

First, think about how *often* you want to monitor your weight. During this 100 Days Program, I recommend that you weigh yourself every day. But if you prefer, you can get on the scale once a week or use whatever time frame works for you.

In addition to using the scale to monitor your progress, notice the changes in how your clothes fit. Take body measurements at intervals, and then calculate the number of inches you've lost. Also, pay attention to all the improvements in your actions, your learning, and your daily personal growth.

For most people, there's no reason to avoid using the scale. But if weighing yourself makes you feel upset or affects your self-esteem, get rid of your scale or hide it in the closet. You might even choose to stay off the scale for the entire 100 Days Program. Do what works best for you.

How to keep yourself going

At the end of each set of 10 lessons, you'll find two divider pages that include a list of the next group of topics. If you ever feel tempted to stop your program, skip to one of these pages, where you'll see the following message:

You've come this far in your 100 days . . .

Don't stop now. If you're struggling to stick with it, push yourself to finish *one more day.* You'll immediately be another day closer to achieving your weight-loss goals.

Just do one more day!

Each time you complete another day on your 100 Days Program, you'll have moved further on the road toward your new life. Remind yourself that you are a valuable and worthwhile person and that you deserve to be at a healthy weight. Stay dedicated to your dream—and *make it a great 100 days!*

TAKE THE CHALLENGE!

Sign up to participate in the 100 Days of Weight Loss Challenge at www.100DaysChallenge.com.

This special challenge is designed to keep you on target with your weight-loss efforts for the entire 100 Days Program. As a member, you'll receive weekly e-mail tips as well as regular teleclasses, bonus materials, and other great resources.

❧ DAYS 1–10 ❧

SET UP FOR SUCCESS

DAY 1   I used to be that way . . .

DAY 2   Interested or committed?

DAY 3   Do it anyway

DAY 4   Boundaries, not diets

DAY 5   Magic notebook

DAY 6   Protect your program

DAY 7   I can do it!

DAY 8   Help me, please . . .

DAY 9   Here's what I want

DAY 10   Appreciate good support

1

❧ DAY 1 ❧

I used to be that way . . .

You are so determined to make this program work. This time you really want to stay on your weight-loss plan and reach your goal. But deep inside, you may be afraid you haven't changed at all and that you'll quit your program long before the 100 days are up.

Perhaps a tiny voice is reminding you of your past failures with dieting. In the beginning, you're always very excited and motivated. But after a few weeks, your enthusiasm drops, and without meaning to, you slip up.

Maybe you sneak an extra candy bar or a bowl of ice cream at the end of a bad day. Then you reason that since you've already blown it, you can go ahead and eat more. Soon you get discouraged with your behavior and eventually you quit your diet completely, just as you always do.

Change your thinking

Stop right there! Your past does *not* determine your future. In fact, your previous failures have absolutely no effect on your ability to succeed now. Starting today, eliminate the belief that things *always* go a certain way or that you *never* stay with your goals. Whenever those doubts creep back in, immediately give yourself this new message:

I used to be that way, but now I'm different!

This powerful statement completely ignores whatever you did before and instead promises you can change your outcome entirely. Rather than being fearful that you'll repeat the past, build a new way of thinking.

Make up a new ending

Because *now you're different*, you can do anything. You can even create different endings for your old negative patterns. Suppose you've been worried because you "always gain your weight back." Come up with a new statement that describes what you can do to prevent this.

For example, you might say, "I used to give up on a diet after a few weeks. But now, I pull out my journal every day and use writing to keep myself on track."

When doubts creep in, remind yourself that *now* you handle life differently. Go ahead and invent entirely new outcomes for your goals, then remind yourself often about your ideas. With time these patterns will become permanent and your dream of success will come true.

TODAY

- Make a list of any fears or negative behaviors that have hurt your weight-loss success in the past. Read each one out loud, and then say, "I used to be that way, but now I'm different."

- Then write new endings for them by completing this sentence: I used to _____ (fill in your old behavior), but now I _____ (write in your new ending).

- Read these new outcomes often, and then live in a way that makes them true.

3

❧ DAY 2 ❧

Interested or committed?

D ebbie was discouraged. "Whenever I start a new diet, I'm so determined to stay on it until I reach my goal. But after just a few weeks, something comes up—a party, someone's birthday—and next thing I know, I slip off my plan and give up."

Do you feel totally determined to stick with your efforts, or do you entertain a few nagging thoughts about "having fun" instead of staying on your plan? If you tend to start and stop every time you diet, you may want to look at the difference between being *interested* and being *committed*.

Interest slips away quickly

With *interested,* you tend to stay with your plans only until something better comes along. For example, you may decide that you're interested in losing weight, but when someone brings doughnuts to work, you quickly go off your diet.

When you're just interested in dieting, you depend on seeing results to keep you on target. So as long as the scale keeps moving, you stay motivated. But if you hit a plateau or you don't see much progress for a few weeks, you may throw your program out the window.

Then when you struggle, you blame everyone but yourself. You accuse your friends of ruining your diet because they eat potato chips in front of you. In addition, you fall into "if only" thinking, saying things like, "If only I had more time, more money, a new job, or a supportive spouse, then I'd be able to stay on my plan."

Committed means "no matter what!"

When you're truly *committed* to achieving your goals, you have an entirely different outlook. Unlike being interested, where it doesn't take much to detract you from your goals, being committed means you stick with it, *no matter what.*

Rather than depending on results to help you stay on track, you work on keeping your motivation strong, knowing that results will follow. You don't blame circumstances or other people for your struggles. Instead, you stay on your diet in spite of not having enough money, time, or supportive friends and family members.

Look carefully at your current efforts. If you tend to easily fall away from your weight-loss plan, decide if you're taking the *interested* approach. If so, strive for being *committed* instead. Start adopting a "no matter what" attitude, then convince yourself you can stay with your goals regardless of your daily challenges.

TODAY

- Decide that you will always be *committed* to your weight-loss plan, not just *interested.*

- In your notebook, describe how you will stick with your program, *no matter what.*

- Do at least one thing today that demonstrates you are truly committed. For example, take a walk or eat your vegetables—*no matter what.*

❦ DAY 3 ❦

Do it anyway

I *don't feel like exercising today!* Does this sound familiar? Then what happens? Do you push yourself and exercise in spite of not feeling like it? Or do you give in and hang out on the couch because you don't *feel* like making the effort?

Right now, you may be solidly committed to your goals. But what happens when you don't *feel* like cooking healthy meals or following your diet plan? If you aren't careful, you can easily slide back from being *committed* to being just *interested.*

Committed means do it anyway

You don't usually wait until you *feel* like going to work. You just go. The same thing is true for visiting your mother or changing dirty diapers. Because you consider these things to be important, you do them regardless of how you feel at the moment.

In the same way, you don't have to feel like working on your weight-loss plan to stick with your program. To improve your commitment, learn to focus on your actions, not just your feelings. On days you're not in the mood for exercising or eating right, tell yourself to *do it anyway.*

Then skip the leftover dessert and eat your fruit instead. Get up off the couch and put on your workout shoes. If you're really committed to your goals, you'll make these choices no matter what, regardless of whether you feel like it or not. Each day, take a few steps that will move you forward, even if you *don't feel* like it. Remember that when you're truly committed, you *do it anyway.*

Here's a summary of the differences between people who are *interested* in their goals compared to those who are *committed*.

People who are interested in losing weight

- Stick with it until something better comes along

- Take action only if they "feel like" doing it

- Need to see results in order to stay motivated

- Blame people or circumstances for their struggles

- Easily give up when they face challenges

People who are committed to losing weight

- Stick with their plans no matter what

- Take action whether they feel like doing it or not

- Assume that if they stay motivated, results will follow

- Take responsibility for their own actions

- Keep going in spite of challenges and setbacks

TODAY

- In your diet or exercise plan, identify a task you don't feel like doing, and then *do it anyway!*

- Notice how it feels to accomplish a goal by taking a "no matter what" approach to it.

- In your notebook, make a list of actions you plan to stick with today, regardless of how you feel at the moment.

❧ DAY 4 ❧

Boundaries, not diets

You've probably heard people say that diets are bad for you and that you should "never diet again!" The problem isn't usually with diets themselves, but with the rigid, perfectionist ways we use them.

If you're like most people, when you're on a diet, you try hard to follow it perfectly. Each day you strive to take in the exact number of calories, fat grams, or carbohydrates allowed by the plan.

But if you slip up and eat a delicious (but forbidden) food, you figure you've blown it, so you might as well eat more. Soon you throw the entire diet out the window. This all-or-nothing approach never works because when you are *off* your diet, you cancel out the progress you made while you were on it.

Boundaries define your diet

Like it or not, to lose weight, you have to follow some type of system. Your plan can be quite rigid and meticulous, or as simple as deciding you'll eat less and increase your level of exercise. Instead of getting stuck on the word *diet*, learn to think of it as setting *boundaries* for your eating plan.

Picture your diet program as a road or a path. You can define the boundaries of your diet road based on the number of calories, points, or other factors you choose to follow. As you walk on the road each day, your goal is to stay between the sides of the road. Unlike strict or rigid diet plans, boundaries stay flexible. They provide guidelines, but at the same time they allow for common sense and good judgment.

During times when you're strong and focused on your diet, you move the boundaries closer together, making the road narrower. When you take a break from your program or work on maintenance, you widen the boundaries and allow more variety in your plan. But even on a really bad day, you never eliminate the road or get off of it completely.

Set guidelines, not rules

Boundaries should give you benefits, not punishment! They should provide guidelines for you to live by, but not burden you with rules. You can define boundaries for any type of diet or weight-loss approach. Depending on your needs, you can simply adjust the edges of your plan to match where you are in life. By doing this, you'll be far more successful than if you punish yourself every time you step off the road.

TODAY

- In your notebook, draw a line down the middle of the page, creating two columns.

- Label one column "Narrow road" for your diet plan. Label the other "Wider road" for your maintenance or alternative eating plan.

- Under the titles, define your eating and exercise plans for each of these roads. Then decide on ways you can be flexible with them without losing sight of the healthy road you want to follow.

DAY 5

Magic notebook

Every night before going to sleep, Judy pulled out a spiral notebook and recorded her thoughts from the day. When she looked back over her progress during the past year, she concluded, "When I journal, I stay on track. It helps me catch the times when I'm slipping into emotional eating or getting discouraged with my efforts. Then I can make changes and correct those issues right away."

Get a "magic" notebook

For many people, recording personal thoughts or actions each day provides valuable insight. It also serves as an outlet for emotions and struggles around weight-loss efforts. If you enjoy writing, experiment with tracking your thoughts and ideas about food and eating. Feel free to write as little as one sentence or as much as several pages.

On the other hand, if you don't find it helpful to write things down, don't force yourself to do this. But do keep a notebook handy as a quick tool for jotting down ideas about managing your eating patterns.

Eat it another time

Just because you think about a food doesn't mean you have to eat it. Whenever Jennifer got a craving for a specific food such as cheesecake, she wrote it in her notebook. She said, "By writing it down, I take it out of my head. I tell myself I don't have to think about it anymore because it's recorded and I can always return to it later."

When a food thought crosses your mind, remind yourself that you don't have to act on it. Instead, write down the name or even a description of the food and then anticipate the pleasure of eating it sometime in the future.

Practice the skill of observing food cues, then letting them go. When you walk into a movie theater, notice the smell of popcorn, and then forget about it. If it helps, record these cues in your "magic" notebook. Tell yourself, "That popcorn smells good, but I'm not going to eat any right now. I'll simply postpone it until another day."

TODAY

- Whenever you think about a particular food you want, write it down in your notebook.

- Plan that you'll eat it at another time. If you wish, add the amount you'll have and how often you'll fit it into your program.

- Stretch the times further apart for eating this food. You may discover that after a while, certain foods don't seem as important to you as they once did.

≈ DAY 6 ≈

Protect your program

No one will ever care as much about your diet plan as you. So it's your job to prevent people or events from pulling you off track. Instead of depending on others to help you be successful with your diet, make a commitment that you will *protect your program at all costs!*

Watch for ways to recognize and avoid situations that might cause you to weaken. Rather than assume you'll be able to resist your mom's apple pie or the potluck casseroles at work, don't put yourself in the situation where you'll have to test your willpower.

"Not just yet . . ."

Here's a great way to protect yourself when you're around other people. Anytime you feel pressured to eat something, you can sidestep the food pusher by hinting that you'll eat later. Whenever someone offers you food, respond by saying, *"Not just yet; I'm going to wait a little while."*

If you're asked again, simply repeat this phrase or another variation of it such as, "Thanks, but I'll still wait a little bit." Saying "not just yet" gives you a gracious way to handle being pushed to eat when you don't want to. Because this magic phrase convinces people you'll eat eventually, they'll leave you alone for the moment.

When you're invited to take seconds or eat dessert, make it sound as if you'll have some later, then quietly slip away from the table. Anytime someone encourages you to eat, such as at baby showers, birthday parties, or other social gatherings, you can use the "not just yet" line again and again. Even if you skip food during the entire event, you'll find that most people never notice you didn't eat.

Don't discuss your "diet"

Often it's best to avoid getting caught up in conversations about dieting and weight loss. When people ask how you're losing weight, simply tell them you're following a *healthy eating program*. You can even respond to their questions by saying, "My weight-loss counselor recommends that we don't discuss the program because talking about food makes us want to eat."

Finally, protect your program during long, empty times such as evenings or weekends when it's easy to start looking for food. Stay occupied by planning activities or pulling out some good books. When you're tempted to give in and eat, recite the words, "I must protect my program at all costs!"

TODAY

- Watch for chances to respond to food invitations by using the line, "Not just yet; I'm going to wait a little while."

- Identify at least three high-risk times or events such as family gatherings or quiet weekends. In your notebook, write down how you'll protect your diet program during each of these.

- Do at least one thing today that reinforces your determination to protect your program at all costs.

☀ DAY 7 ☀
I can do it!

Whew! You've made it through the first week! How do you feel right now? A bit excited? Hopeful? Scared? You probably feel some level of all of these. If you've struggled with your weight in the past, you may also be afraid you'll repeat your same old patterns.

Kick those thoughts away! For the moment, squash your doubts about staying on your diet and exercise plan. Today you are strong! You're invincible! And nothing can stop you! This time, you're going to do it!

Become your own cheerleader

To increase your success with this program, skyrocket your self-talk and create a strong belief you *can* do this. Become your own cheerleader, shouting out words of encouragement that will keep your motivation strong every single day.

To enhance your cheerleading, think about *why* you are so convinced you can be successful. Invent several phrases that reinforce your determination to stay on your plan for at least 100 days. Here are a few ideas to get you started:

- I'm totally determined.

- I've done it before and I can do it again.

- I'm using a great weight-loss plan.

- I'm capable of accomplishing anything.

- Others have done it and so can I!

Recite these phrases every day, using them to reinforce your determination to make this program work.

Inspire yourself

Have you read any real-life stories about people who have lost a lot of weight and also maintained their success? Draw from these examples as well as from friends or colleagues who have accomplished phenomenal goals. Let these people inspire you and help keep you motivated to stick with your efforts. Tell yourself, "If they can do it, so can I."

Practice saying the words "I can do it!" over and over. Write them on sticky notes, and then post them on your mirror, your computer screen, and your car dash. Read them many times a day, maybe even 100 times. Push them deep into your mind and use them as a powerful affirmation that you *will* succeed with your plan.

TODAY

- Tell yourself "I can do it" at least 10 times. Use this to cheerlead yourself through the entire day!

- In your notebook, write "I can do it because . . ." and then add a few supportive phrases such as "I'm capable of doing anything."

- Read your phrases often, using them to reinforce your goals and build your enthusiasm.

🌿 DAY 8 🌿

Help me, please . . .

Do you ever wish you could get more support from people around you? If only the "helpers" in your life knew exactly what you wanted them to say! Unfortunately, they don't. In fact, sometimes they just make things worse.

With good intentions, people grab cookies out of your hand as they scold, "Should you be eating that?" Or they ignore you and don't say anything, even when you wear much smaller clothes or weigh 30 pounds less than you did a few months ago.

Decide what you want

To get support instead of criticism from the people you love, you may have to *train* them. Instead of begging, "Please help me lose weight" or "Be nicer to me," clarify exactly what you mean by those words, and then be more specific in your requests.

Decide what type of support you truly need. Do you want words of encouragement? Silence? Help with cooking meals? Instead of being angry or frustrated because people don't do these things, let them know how they can help you.

Speak up about the challenges of leftovers or open pizza boxes. Maybe you wish family members would eat their snacks in another room instead of in front of you. If so, then tell them.

Set up agreements with your support people by saying, "It will help me if . . ." followed by what you want them to do. For example, you might say, "It will help me a lot if we don't have potato chips in the house right now. Would you be willing to eat them at work instead of bringing them home?"

Please don't say this . . .

Be sure you also let people know the things you *don't want* them to do or say. For example, do you enjoy being praised or having people comment on your progress? Or would you prefer they not say anything about your weight or your looks right now?

Let people know which type of comments feel good to you compared to the ones that make you feel uncomfortable. Also tell them about specific phrases that set you off. For example, maybe you don't ever want family members to ask, "Is that on your diet?" Decide what you'd like to hear instead and let them know.

TODAY

- In your journal, write a list of things that people are *always* welcome to say or do in regard to your weight-loss efforts. Examples might include: offer you compliments, protect you from dessert, or clear the table after meals.

- Create another list of things you *don't* ever want people to do, such as: snatch your plate away, give you lectures, or admonish, "You're not supposed to be eating that."

- Read both lists to your support people including your spouse, your children, and your best friend.

❧ DAY 9 ❧

Here's what I want

Today you'll discover the secret to getting exactly what you want from all the support people in your life. But before you're able to let others know how to provide support and encouragement, you first have to decide what you want.

In the quiz below, pick out the answers that fit best for you. Think carefully about your true preferences. Decide what motivates you as well as what frustrates you. If the answers don't exactly fit for you, come up with some different ones that match your needs.

WHAT I WANT FROM YOU

1. *If you see me eating something that's not on my diet plan*
   ___ Ask me, "Should you be eating that?"
   ___ Ignore it entirely.
   ___ Ask me if I've had a bad day.
   ___ Give me a hug.

2. *When I'm making progress, such as losing weight*
   ___ Compliment me on how I look.
   ___ Praise me in front of others.
   ___ Never comment on my progress in front of others.
   ___ Give me non-food gifts or rewards.

3. *When I'm struggling or gaining weight*
   ___ Tell me you notice and really care about my struggle.

___ Ignore it entirely.

___ Hug me and show me extra affection.

___ Ask me how you can help.

4. *When I'm making progress you can't see (such as improving my self-esteem)*

___ Ask me how my efforts are going.

___ Compliment me on how I look.

___ Ignore my efforts and my changes.

___ Give me non-food gifts or rewards.

5. *When I've maintained my weight (even though I may still want to lose more)*

___ Tell me you are proud of my current efforts.

___ Ignore the subject entirely.

___ Ask me if I'm struggling or feeling discouraged.

___ Compliment me on my looks and my efforts.

TODAY

- Complete this quiz, and then read your answers out loud to one of your support people such as your spouse or a good friend.

- Post your answers on your refrigerator or in some other location where your support people can be reminded of what you want.

- Write the most important answers in your journal for future reference.

⚜ DAY 10 ⚜
Appreciate good support

Getting support from others involves give and take. When people give you solid, helpful support, let them know you appreciate it. Be willing to talk about your goals and your plans for achieving them. Take time to share some of the stories about your progress, especially in areas that don't involve the numbers on the scale.

Remind people that what they can see is only a small part of your plan. Then tell them about what they *can't see*—how you've curbed your emotional eating, stopped the McDonald's run on the way home from work, and eliminated all of your extra snacks.

Learn to receive compliments

Do you feel uncomfortable when you get noticed? If so, you may need to practice the art of accepting compliments and praise more graciously. It's easy to discount people's comments because of your own frustrations or opinions. But when you react to compliments in a negative way, it makes people think their support doesn't mean anything to you.

When someone offers you a genuine comment about your progress, try to respond warmly to the person who pays you the compliment. For example, if people remark that you look great because you've lost weight, don't minimize their words by saying, "Yes, but I still have such a long way to go."

Instead, use your response to affirm and appreciate the other person by saying something such as, "You can't imagine how much it means to hear you say that. Thank you!"

Don't set them up

Avoid hooking people with awkward questions that they can't answer honestly. Here are some examples:

- Does this dress make me look fat?

- Can you tell if I've lost any weight?

- Does my fat stomach bother you?

People hate these questions! They know you'll probably get upset with their answers or you'll even accuse them of not telling the truth. If you feel insecure or you struggle with your self-esteem, focus on dealing with these issues instead of punishing your support team.

During times when people get impatient about your progress, guide them on how to support you when you aren't doing well. Let them know it's not their fault—they aren't responsible for the changes you're making in your life. Simply appreciate their concern by saying, "It's so nice to know that you'll be here for me when I'm ready to work on this."

TODAY

- Ask a friend or family member to compliment you on anything from your weight loss to your hair or your clothes.

- Come up with a response that affirms the person who gave you the compliment. For example, you might say, "You really made my day by telling me that! Thank you so much."

- Record your favorite responses in your notebook.

DAYS 1–10 COMPLETED!

You've come this far in your 100 days . . .

Don't stop now. If you're struggling to stick with it, push yourself to finish *one more day.* You'll immediately be another day closer to achieving your weight-loss goals.

Just do one more day!

❧ DAYS 11–20 ❧

PUT FOOD IN ITS PLACE

DAY 11   Two purposes of food

DAY 12   Fuel or filler

DAY 13   Oops, I forgot to eat!

DAY 14   Morning affects evening

DAY 15   First two bites

DAY 16   Nurturing power of food

DAY 17   Stop wasting food

DAY 18   Retrain eating habits

DAY 19   Eat reasonable amounts

DAY 20   Half-off special

❧ DAY 11 ❧

Two purposes of food

Food is wonderful! And you can absolutely enjoy food and eating, yet still manage your weight. But in order to be successful with this, you need to put food in its proper place.

From now on, plan that you will eat for only two reasons:

1. To fuel your body

2. To appreciate flavors

Measure your food intake against these guidelines. If you put something in your mouth and it doesn't match either of these, there's a good chance you're doing emotional eating.

Make fuel a priority

In the days ahead, you'll learn new ways to enjoy food and appreciate flavors without adding lots of calories. But for now, focus on making your fuel needs a high priority. Just as a car needs gas, your body requires fuel to keep it moving efficiently. And to get the best mileage, you need to fill your tank at intervals, stop when it's full, and use high-quality fuel.

Plan for a minimum of three fuel stops a day, then add a couple of mini-stops in between. You don't need to eat a lot at each fueling. In fact, you may want to space out your fuel intake by eating five or six small meals each day.

Just be sure that you always give your body fuel when it needs it. Even when your days are filled with demands such as work deadlines or taking kids to ball practices, don't ignore your fuel needs. Take food along if necessary so you don't get stuck with running on empty.

Eat more often

My friend Jorge Cruise, author of *The 3-Hour Diet* and the *Eight Minutes in the Morning* book series, believes that eating more frequently gives much better weight-loss results. His work shows that getting consistent fuel intake helps protect metabolism as well as maintain blood-sugar levels. It also prevents you from overeating as a result of getting too hungry or tired.

Regardless of what type of diet and exercise plan you're on, always make sure to give your body fuel at regular intervals. Over the long run, you will see far better success than if you skimp on the fuel you need.

TODAY

- Each time you eat something, write down the time that you ate it. Include all of your meals as well as snacks and nibbles. At the end of the day, count the number of times you took in fuel.

- Plan ways to space your fuel stops between three to four hours apart.

- Notice whether having regular fuel stops during the day improves your energy and your focus.

☘ DAY 12 ☘
Fuel or filler

Take a close look at the foods you eat most. Are you getting adequate amounts of fuel? Or do you keep adding filler to your tank? Keep in mind that fuel keeps your body running, but filler often gets sent directly to your fat stores.

Quality fuel provides solid nutritional content, with limited amounts of fat, sugar, and empty calories. Generally you get decent fuel from most healthy foods, such as low-fat meats, fruits, vegetables, and whole grains.

Filler foods tend to add extra calories but provide minimal nutrients. Most sweets, chips, and snack foods fit into this category. When you constantly fill your tank with easy-to-grab snacks such as cookies or chips, it's hard to get good mileage from your body.

Even with healthy foods, watch to be sure that you're getting quality fuel. Sometimes what starts out as fuel turns into filler. For example, a bakery muffin typically has the same amount of sugar and fat as a large cupcake. And when you pour extra dressing on your salad, you dilute all of the fuel benefits of the salad greens and vegetables.

Filler drains energy

Don't ask your body to run on junk. Filler usually harms your energy as well as your weight-loss efforts. When you reach for snacks or desserts that you know are filler, limit yourself to small amounts. Focus on appreciating the tastes of these foods rather than using them as your main fuel source for the day.

To improve the quality of your fuel intake, look for foods with significant nutrient density. For salads, use dark-colored greens such as spinach and add lots of vegetables. Expand your fuel list by trying less common but healthy foods such as kiwi, jicama, kale, or mangoes.

Plan your fuel

Never assume you can get healthy food at a moment's notice. To avoid getting trapped without fuel, pack your own meals for airplane or road trips. Carry a protein bar with you when you go shopping. If you'll be spending most of your day in meetings, bring along a fuel kit that contains healthy snacks such as fruit and a container of yogurt.

TODAY

- Record each of the foods you eat today, then rate each one based on whether it provides fuel or filler.

- At the end of the day, determine how well your fuel needs were met.

- Decide whether you need to replace some filler items with healthy foods that provide more fuel.

❧ DAY 13 ❧

Oops, I forgot to eat!

It's been a crazy day. You've attended meetings, answered numerous telephone calls and e-mails, and then pushed to meet the deadline on a major project. Suddenly you look up at the clock and realize you completely missed lunch.

Now you're famished, so you eat whatever you can get your hands on quickly. Often that ends up being a candy bar or a small handful of nuts from your desk drawer. So much for getting quality fuel!

Skipping meals might sound like an easy way to lose weight. But it rarely works because your body outsmarts your plan. Whenever you go long periods without fuel, your body protects itself by hoarding some of the calories for later use. You also risk getting a late-day energy slump, which leads to even more eating struggles.

Saving up calories

When Susan knows she's having a big dinner at night, she avoids eating all day. In her mind she's saving up the calories so she'll have room for her favorite foods. Unfortunately this pattern tends to do the opposite of what Susan intended.

In reality our bodies know how to manage fuel sources very efficiently. When you undereat during the day, your body believes it may not get enough food, so it conserves what does come in. Even if Susan eats the same total number of calories as usual, her body will store a portion of that large evening meal, causing her to gain weight.

In the same way, if you routinely follow a one-meal-a-day plan, your body will train itself to get by on a small amount of food. Eventually it adapts so well to the low-calorie level that it refuses to lose weight.

You have no choice

During the years when I was working in hospitals, I knew a diabetic nurse named Ellen. While the rest of us complained that we couldn't stop for lunch, Ellen always found time to eat her meals and snacks. She said, "I don't have a choice. If I don't eat, I'll pass out and I won't be any help at all."

You don't have to be diabetic to use this strategy. Just make it a habit to tell yourself, "I have no choice." By convincing yourself that skipping meals is *not* an option, you'll work a lot harder to routinely take care of your fuel needs.

TODAY

- Write down the times of the day when you plan to eat your meals and snacks.

- Make an effort to eat within 30 minutes of these scheduled times. At the end of the day, review your eating patterns to see how well you did.

- If you tend to skip meals or forget to eat, set an alarm to remind yourself when it's time for fuel.

✻ DAY 14 ✻

Morning affects evening

D o you ever start munching late in the day, then snack your way through the rest of the afternoon and the evening? If you have problems with late-day eating, take a look at what you did earlier in the day. Often struggles with hunger, fatigue, and food cravings in the afternoon or evening relate to how you ate in the morning.

Breakfast and hunger

Are you usually a breakfast eater? Or do you avoid eating in the mornings because it seems to make you feel hungry all day? When you routinely skip breakfast, your digestive tract stays dormant until you finally give it food.

If you surprise your stomach one morning by unexpectedly eating breakfast, it secretes more digestive acid than the food requires, causing hunger pangs to linger for several hours.

Don't skip breakfast in an attempt to avoid this struggle with hunger. If you eat breakfast *every day,* you'll eventually retrain your stomach to manage food better in the mornings. It may take time for your body to adjust, but after a week on your new schedule, your all-day hunger will disappear.

You also may need to evaluate the timing of your fuel stops and begin eating more often. When you don't give your body enough fuel during the early part of the day, by late in the afternoon, it starts screaming for food.

Worse yet, your system may have a hard time catching up. This can make you keep nibbling all evening, even after you've eaten a large dinner.

Afternoon droop

Are you often famished and exhausted when you get home from work? By this time of day, fatigue and hunger can easily ruin your judgment about eating. To manage this late-day, high-risk time, *always* eat a snack sometime between three and four o'clock in the afternoon.

Look for healthy fuel sources that include both protein and carbohydrates. For example, you might have an apple along with a mozzarella cheese stick or combine a few slices of deli turkey with some raw vegetables. Many of the commercial energy bars also contain a good balance of both nutrients. The protein in the food will slow down the digestive process, giving you a long-lasting energy boost from the snack.

TODAY

- Set a goal of eating breakfast every day for the next week. In your notebook, record what you ate.

- If you wish, you can split your breakfast into two mini-meals and eat the second one mid-morning.

- Plan a couple of options for late-afternoon snacks. List them in your notebook so you'll remember your ideas.

❧ DAY 15 ❧
First two bites

Picture your favorite dessert on the table in front of you. Maybe it's a piece of your mom's homemade apple pie, a slice of turtle cheesecake, or a bowl of rocky road ice cream.

As you take the first bite, you swoon with pleasure. Wow, is this ever good! Excited to have more, you reach for another bite, marveling at how great it tastes.

More bites, then still more, and soon it's gone. But did you really notice the rest of the food? Initially, you appreciated its flavor and texture, but then you stopped paying attention and simply ate until you finished it off.

Power of the first two bites

You may not realize it, but the *first two bites* of any food will always have the most flavor. If you keep eating after that, you're just "feeding." Of course, if you're physically hungry, eating more of the food serves a purpose.

But if you want to appreciate the flavor, be aware that no matter how much you eat, the taste won't get any more wonderful than those first two bites. Instead of always taking in many extra calories, why not take advantage of the way your taste buds work?

With any food that you love, eat the first two bites very slowly, noticing details such as the cinnamon in the apple pie or the soft caramel swirl in the cheesecake. Close your eyes and delight in the taste. Allow yourself to completely absorb the texture and flavor of the food.

Is it worth eating more?

After you finish those two bites, decide if you truly need more. In most cases you don't. Once in a while, a food will taste so phenomenal that it's worth the mountain of calories and fat grams it contains. But in reality, very few types of candy, cookies, or even cheesecake fit into that category.

Suppose you're eating one of your favorite desserts such as a chocolate brownie. When you really pay close attention to the taste, you may decide this one isn't as special as you'd anticipated. If that's the case, stop eating. Tell yourself you've gotten what you needed from it. Then either toss or give away the rest so you aren't tempted to eat something that isn't all that great.

TODAY

- Choose one of your favorite foods such as carrot cake, and then focus on all the details and tastes of the first two bites. Let yourself appreciate the flavors.

- After the first two bites, stop eating and get rid of the rest of the food. In your notebook, write down the details about this experience.

- With each food you eat today, pay close attention to the first two bites. Notice how they taste in comparison to the rest of the food.

✿ DAY 16 ✿

Nurturing power of food

When you're feeling stressed or sad or lonely, food does seem to make you feel better. At least initially, it calms your anger or anxiety and lifts your spirits. But how long does food keep working?

As you know, the first two bites of any food have the most impact on your taste buds. But they're also the only ones that have any *emotional power!* After you finish those first bites, you'll have received whatever benefits the food has for you. Eating more of it simply won't bring you additional satisfaction or make you feel any better.

You're done!

After a long, stressful day, Kathy grabbed a pint of chocolate cherry ice cream from the freezer and then sank into her couch. As she ate the ice cream straight from the carton, she kept thinking, "Maybe this is the bite that will do it." Of course, it didn't work. She just felt worse.

If you're eating as a way to feel nurtured or calmed, you'll usually experience some level of those feelings right away. But continuing to eat won't bring any more satisfaction or make you feel better. In fact, at some point you'll probably begin to feel frustrated and disappointed with your behavior instead of being healed by the food.

Once you understand that eating more won't continue to improve your emotional state, you can use this in your favor.

With a little effort, you can train yourself to feel better after eating only a small amount of nurturing food.

Letting food work

In weight-loss seminars, I often hand out small chocolate-chip cookies. Then I invite class participants to eat *two bites* of their cookies while allowing themselves to feel nurtured and emotionally soothed by them.

After they finish those first two bites, I ask them to throw away the remainder of their cookies. Some people can hardly bear to do this. Yet at the same time, they admit those two bites were completely satisfying, and they really don't need to eat any more.

TODAY

- Intentionally eat something that will help you feel better. Soak up the pleasure from a delicious piece of chocolate. Allow yourself the comfort of eating your favorite ice cream or a luscious cinnamon roll. Eliminate any thoughts of guilt or remorse as you eat this food.

- *After two bites, stop!* Remind yourself that your needs have been met and eating more of the food won't increase your healing level. Then give away or toss whatever food is left.

- Write about how you felt doing this exercise. Also, notice what level of satisfaction you experienced as you ate the first two bites of the food.

☘ DAY 17 ☘
Stop wasting food

D o you tend to always clean your plate? As a child, were you told you should never waste food? Unfortunately, old rules about eating all of your food can ruin your diet plan.

Think about where you first heard those clean-your-plate messages. When you were growing up, did people around you cringe if food was wasted? Were you praised for eating it all? Maybe you were taught that leaving food behind wasn't fair to the starving children in the world.

Of course, not wasting food makes total sense. In some cases you can prevent having too much food in the first place by cooking smaller amounts or sharing meals at restaurants. But even with careful planning, sometimes you'll be stuck with extra food you don't need. Eventually you have to learn to manage leftovers without eating all of them.

It's wasted anyway

The eat-it-all rule is one of the hardest ones for most people to break. But when you fill your car with gas, you don't keep pumping after the tank is full, spilling the fuel on the ground. So why would you do that with your body?

Here's a new way to look at those old rules about cleaning your plate:

Every time you eat food your body doesn't need,
you are wasting it!

So now you have a choice. You can get rid of leftover food by throwing it away or by eating it. Either way, it's wasted.

Eating your child's leftovers

The same thing is true when your children leave food behind. Certainly it's important to teach kids a sense of responsibility around food. But often they simply take more than they can finish. If you can't bear to throw away their leftovers, just remind yourself that *if you eat it, the food is wasted.*

Starting today, make a commitment that you will not waste food by putting it into your body. This mental shift may not come easily. But if you're serious about managing your weight, you have to let go of cleaning your plate. If you can't do this, you'll probably continue to struggle with reaching your goals.

TODAY

- Throw some food away. It can be a tiny amount or a large amount. Remember, by wasting it into the garbage, you're not wasting it into yourself.

- In your journal, list the foods you let go of today. Make a note about how it felt to throw food away, then add a few thoughts on how you'll manage leftover food in the future.

- Write down a few ways you can prevent having excess food around in the first place.

❦ DAY 18 ❦
Retrain eating habits

If you've lived by the clean-your-plate rule for a long time, you may continue to struggle with the idea of throwing food away. If so, focus on how to stop giving food so much power that you can't leave some of it behind. Remember that your weight and your health are always more important than a leftover piece of pie.

One pea at a time

If you can't bring yourself to throw away what's left on your plate, retrain yourself gradually by leaving one small piece of food at a time. Jan was raised in a family that had strict rules about never throwing food away. As an adult she couldn't let go of this pattern, even though it caused her to overeat.

One evening at dinner, Jan decided to leave one green pea on her plate. Each of the next several nights, she left a little bit of food on her plate, increasing the amount each time by the size of a pea. Eventually she broke her habit of feeling anxious or guilty if she didn't clean her plate.

The restaurant trap

Starting at home, intentionally leave some food behind at every meal. After you're comfortable doing this, apply the same concept to restaurant meals.

Of course, you can always take leftover food home and use it for a meal the next day. But be careful with this because it doesn't always accomplish what you planned.

Restaurant meals are often higher in fat and calories than what you might ordinarily eat. When you take your leftovers home, you often end up eating excess calories twice.

If you want to get two meals out of your restaurant food, make sure you select items that match your healthy eating goals. When you decide to eat food that's not quite as healthy, enjoy the taste of your meal while you're at the restaurant, and then leave the rest behind.

TODAY

- Think about all the places you've heard messages related to cleaning your plate. Recall any family members, school lunches, restaurant staff, even strangers who glared if you left food behind. Tell yourself these old clean-your-plate messages no longer apply to your life.

- In your notebook, write some *"Never clean your plate"* rules that show your new attitude.

- For example, one new message might be, "Never clean your plate. Instead, take care of your body and your health, and then figure out other ways to help those around you."

❈ DAY 19 ❈

Eat reasonable amounts

Do you know how much food you should be eating? What equals a *serving?* If you're following a specific diet plan, you need to know whether you're matching the program's guidelines. And at social gatherings where food is served family-style, you need ways to estimate serving sizes so you don't put too much on your plate to begin with.

Start by making sure that you know how to measure foods accurately. It doesn't matter if you're counting calories, fat grams, or carbohydrates. You still have to know how many chips are in one ounce or what a half-cup of pasta looks like. Instead of taking the amount you think is right, practice your estimating skills by comparing your serving with the real thing.

Accurate guessing

Place what you think is a half-cup of cereal or pasta into a bowl. Then pour the food into a measuring cup to see if you're right.

With snack foods, pick up the amount you would guess equals one ounce. Then check your accuracy by using a food scale. You might also want to count out the exact number of nuts or chips in a one-ounce serving so you'll know for the next time.

Serving sizes have a way of growing with time. Every once in a while, pull out your scale and your measuring cups again. Check your estimates to make sure an ounce of cheese hasn't doubled or that a cup of ice cream hasn't become a pint.

Use your palm

In places where you don't have the option of weighing or measuring food, use the palm of your hand to determine the right amount. Because it correlates with body build, your palm gives an accurate way to gauge serving sizes.

For example, the correct serving of meat (anywhere from three to six ounces) is usually the amount that's exactly the size of your palm. With snack foods such as nuts or chips, a typical serving is the amount you can hold loosely in one hand. If you reach for more, you've taken another serving.

TODAY

- With each of the foods you eat today, take the amount you think is your designated serving size. Then weigh or measure the food and see how close you came to being correct.

- Repeat this exercise until you are confident about your estimating skills.

- In your notebook, write down your ideal serving size for the food items you eat most frequently.

❧ DAY 20 ❧
Half-off special

When you are the cook, you can usually take charge of your serving amounts. But away from home, this becomes much more difficult. You need an easy but accurate way to monitor your food intake when you can't measure anything.

Divide and conquer!

For an easy way to manage your serving sizes on an ongoing basis, use a concept called the *half-off special*. That simply means eat half as much as you normally would, or take half of the amount you want.

For example, when you're having lasagna, picture the large serving you'd usually eat, then take half that much. If you want a cookie, divide it into two pieces and then eat only one of them.

At lunchtime, cut your usual sandwich in half and then add a piece of fruit to complete your meal. If you don't feel totally satisfied after eating half a sandwich, save the rest of it for at least two hours and then decide if you still need it.

The "half-off" approach works especially well at banquets or meals that involve several courses. By eating half of each food item, you get to appreciate all of the tastes but don't leave the table feeling stuffed.

Here are a few more ideas for monitoring serving amounts. Decide you won't go back for seconds—ever. Even when you're at family-style dinners or buffets, take food only once. If you crave seconds, you're probably hooked on the taste of the food rather than needing more fuel.

With foods such as pizza or snack items, determine your serving size before you begin eating. Unless you are extremely active, a good serving amount for pizza is two slices if you're female, three if you're male.

Don't worry about whether it's a medium or a large pizza. By setting a limit on the number of slices, you've got a built-in measurement for every size and type. If you're still hungry after finishing your designated serving, reach for a salad or a few raw vegetables instead of more pizza.

Hunger or emotions?

Sometimes the "half-off" concept may feel awkward and even unsatisfying. If you try eating half of your food but you can't stop yourself from finishing it off, take a close look at your emotional needs. Maybe something else in your life requires attention or needs to be *filled*.

You'll learn more about emotional eating in the days ahead. For now, learn to recognize whether it's your body or your head that still wants food. Then take care of what really needs to be addressed.

TODAY

- Divide several of your food items in half, then eat only that much.

- Do this half-off special with at least five foods.

- In your journal, record the foods you ate along with how it felt to leave half of the food behind.

DAYS 11–20 COMPLETED!

You've come this far in your 100 days . . .

Don't stop now. If you're struggling to stick with it, push yourself to finish *one more day.* You'll immediately be another day closer to achieving your weight-loss goals.

Just do one more day!

❧ DAYS 21–30 ❧

CONSCIOUS EATING

⚘ DAY 21 ⚘

Eat with awareness

Have you ever eaten a candy bar, and then wondered where it went? Maybe you've looked down at your plate and had no memory of eating your meal. You can do a lot of damage with this level of unconscious eating and sometimes not even realize it's contributing to your weight gain.

No awareness

Bob had developed the habit of doing many things at the same time. While he was eating dinner, he would read the paper, watch the news on TV, and try to talk with his family.

Often Bob would finish eating his entire meal and wouldn't even realize it! His family members always laughed when he began searching for the bread he'd already eaten, exclaiming, "Who ate my biscuit?"

Remember, there are two purposes for eating—*to fuel your body* and *to appreciate flavors*. When you're eating for fuel, staying conscious helps you become aware of when your tank is full. And if your goal is to appreciate flavors, you certainly want to notice and enjoy the taste of the food you eat.

Slow down

Take a look at your typical eating patterns. Like Bob, are you guilty of eating without awareness? Do you go through the drive-up window at a fast-food restaurant and then devour a sandwich as you drive? You might believe that you're saving time, but often you don't notice the taste of the food or even the fact that you're eating at all.

When you eat with no awareness, you miss out on the flavor, texture, and sensation of your food. Because you didn't "get" the taste you wanted, you may still yearn for it, so you eat more.

Unfortunately, fast eating tends to be unconscious eating, putting you at risk for way too much food. Train yourself to slow down and spend more time with your food rather than wolfing it down on the run.

It takes practice to pay attention when you're eating. But after you cultivate more awareness of the food you eat, you'll discover a new level of appreciation and enjoyment.

TODAY

- Prepare yourself for having a "mindful-eating" meal by setting a table with your good china and silverware, lighting a candle, and playing quiet music in the background.

- Sit down for your meal. While you're eating, don't do any other activities—focus entirely on the food. Notice details such as the food's appearance, flavors and textures, and even the temperature.

- In your notebook, record your observations. Then add a few notes about how it feels to eat a meal using that much focus and total awareness.

✤ DAY 22 ✤

Multitask with food

To eat with awareness, you have to pay attention to what's in front of you. But that doesn't mean you can't focus on other things as well. If you're like most people, you probably multitask by working on the computer, talking on the phone, and doing laundry all at the same time.

Remember that you're eating

You don't have to completely avoid doing anything else in order to stay conscious around food. But you do have to pay attention to your actions. If you're doing other activities at the same time, remind yourself that *you are eating* and stay aware of what you put in your mouth.

Like having a two-year-old child in your house, you can learn to stay on constant alert even while you're busy with other things. With a little practice, you can stay focused on your food at the same time you engage in conversations or enjoy entertainment.

If you choose to eat while you're watching movies or TV, don't become oblivious to your food. Instead, learn to divide your attention between the screen and your plate.

Awareness training

Here's a great exercise for improving awareness around food. Choose a meal, snack, or even a piece of fruit, and then sit down with it on a plate in front of you. Study the food for a minute or two. Breathe in the smell, observe the colors, and notice the patterns in the food.

Then take a bite, paying attention to the flavor, the texture, and the way it feels in your mouth. Chew it slowly and let yourself fully enjoy the experience of eating.

Now look for ways to challenge your awareness. Take a large bite and swallow it quickly, pretending you're on the run. Next, pick up the plate and carry it around the room. Eat a few bites while you watch TV or look outdoors. Then sit back down and focus entirely on the food again.

Notice that when you work at it, you're able to maintain total awareness of your food, regardless of the situation. Repeat this exercise a few times until you're able to stay focused on eating, no matter what's going on around you.

TODAY

- Do a conscious eating exercise with someone such as your spouse, a friend, or one of your children.

- Intentionally create several distractions such as watching TV or having a conversation, but remain totally aware of your food intake.

- Write a few sentences in your journal to describe what you learned from this experience.

❧ DAY 23 ❧

Savoring

A nother way you can increase awareness of your food is to use the concept of *savoring*. With this technique, you eat a very small amount at a time. But while you're eating, you pay total attention to how the food tastes and feels.

Learning to savor

To practice savoring, choose a piece of chocolate or other type of candy that you can eat in five or six tiny bites. One of the best options for this exercise is the Andes brand three-layer, rectangular mint.

Slowly unwrap your candy. Smell it and notice its delicious aroma. When you're ready, bite off one of the four corners. Then one at a time, carefully bite off each of the other three. As you eat, notice the texture and how the candy feels in your mouth. If you're eating an Andes mint or a similar candy, pay special attention to the separate flavors of chocolate and mint.

Next, eat half of what's left, and then finish eating the rest of it. You should have taken a total of six bites from your candy. As you eat the last bite, focus on the sensation of swallowing. Picture the bites moving down your throat and into your stomach. Let yourself *feel* the candy as well as taste it.

One is enough

After you've finished this exercise, ask yourself if you want another mint. Usually the answer is no. When you eat with this level of awareness, you receive an amazing amount of enjoyment and satisfaction from your food.

Also, because you truly notice and appreciate the taste of the food, you get what you want, your craving stops, and you realize that you don't need to eat any more.

Next time you eat one of your favorite foods such as a piece of cheesecake or something chocolate, savor it and notice every detail. Take tiny bites—about the size of a fourth of a teaspoon—and then pay total attention as you eat the food. With each bite, allow yourself to feel contented and satisfied.

You can use this savoring technique with any type of food. It works especially well with sweets and desserts, but it can also give you a new appreciation for foods such as pasta or green beans.

TODAY

- Choose something to savor, ideally an Andes mint or a small square chocolate candy. As you eat, pay attention to the smell, the taste, and the texture as well as the sensation of swallowing it.

- In your notebook, describe what the candy tasted like as well as how it felt in your mouth.

- When you've finished, decide if you need more food or if you're content with what you ate.

❧ DAY 24 ❧
Eat for satisfaction

Do you usually feel completely satisfied with food—or do you continue eating, hoping for just a little more happiness or enjoyment? Do you ever finish one food and then search for something else because you still want to eat?

If you typically reach for another bite or a second handful before you finish the first one, your food can't do its job. For your brain to achieve satisfaction, you have to eat slowly, pay attention to the bites, and appreciate your food.

Let the food in

Imagine drinking a delicious cup of coffee, tea, or hot chocolate. As you sip on this hot beverage, you smile with pleasure. The drink feels very soothing and nurturing, even comforting. This special treat reaches your soul, helping you feel relaxed and fulfilled.

Eating works the same way. If you're determined you want to appreciate flavors, work on getting satisfaction from your food, not guilt or remorse. To do this, you don't have to eat large amounts—you simply have to let the food sink into your awareness. In other words, to feel satisfied by food, you have to be able to "get it."

Savoring your food will help you feel satisfied. But sometimes you have to take it a step further and be willing to allow yourself a sense of pleasure from eating.

When you give yourself permission to enjoy food instead of feeling guilty about eating it, you'll get the satisfaction you crave and you won't have to hunt for something more to eat.

What do you really want?

Michelle had read that to overcome food cravings, she should go ahead and eat the food she wanted. But she couldn't seem to get this concept to work.

"One afternoon I was craving a brownie, so I ate one. After I finished it, I decided that it wasn't quite what I'd wanted. Instead, I was actually hungry for Oreo cookies. After eating several cookies, I sensed they weren't exactly what I wanted either.

Then I figured out what I was really craving was something crunchy like M&M's. So I got out a bag of those and finished them off, but that still didn't quite do it. I don't understand why using the principle of 'eat what you want' doesn't make me feel satisfied."

Michelle's problem with not feeling satisfied wasn't related to food. Instead, what she probably wanted was to feel nurtured or appreciated or some other type of emotion. When you need emotional soothing, eating can often make you feel frustrated rather than healed.

TODAY

- Recall a food or type of meal that's usually highly satisfying for you.

- Write a few words or sentences that describe how it feels to be satisfied by food.

- Eat at least one thing today with the intention of feeling satisfied. Appreciate the food and allow yourself to feel totally fulfilled by eating it.

❧ DAY 25 ❧
Smaller amounts, less often

Contrary to what you might think, you don't need to stop eating all of your favorite foods in order to manage your weight. Instead of avoiding yummy treats such as ice cream or chocolate-chip cookies, plan them into your program. But do it with this special guideline:

Smaller amounts, less often

Think about a favorite food, such as ice cream, that gets you into trouble. First, decide how much is a *smaller amount*. If you typically eat a large bowl of ice cream every night, you might decrease the amount to one-half cup, or a small cone at the ice cream shop. Then determine *how often* you'll eat ice cream, perhaps every Friday instead of nightly.

Avoid feeling deprived

After you've planned a favorite food such as ice cream into your diet, you can look forward to it all week. Because you know you eventually get to have it, you won't be as likely to feel deprived or left out.

Sandra loved barbecued ribs. But every time she started a new diet, she figured she wouldn't get to eat them again for months. So she'd go to her favorite restaurant and eat a pound of ribs. Of course, as soon as her diet floundered, she'd reward herself by eating ribs again.

Using the principle of *smaller amounts, less often,* Sandra decided to eat her favorite ribs only once a month and limit her serving to one-fourth pound.

At the end of the first month, she went to the restaurant, ate the ribs, and really loved her dinner. The next month, Sandra again looked forward to her special night, but this time she noticed the ribs didn't taste quite as good as they had before. By the third month, she didn't seem to crave them anymore, so she decided to eat chicken instead.

You're in charge

Because you love your favorite foods so much, it's easy to give them a lot of power. But this allows food to control your diet, and sometimes, your life. When you plan specific times and amounts for eating what you love, you get back to being in charge of the food, not the other way around.

By using the guideline of *smaller amounts, less often,* you can look forward to eating wonderful foods. Knowing you'll get to enjoy them again in the future will also help you manage the amounts of these foods instead of overeating.

TODAY

- Write a list of your favorite foods. Put as many on the list as you want.

- Choose three of the best ones and write a plan for eating these foods in *smaller amounts, less often.* Be specific about when and how much you'll eat.

- If you wish, record the days and amounts on a calendar. For example, you might decide you'll eat bacon every Saturday, but limit it to two strips.

❧ DAY 26 ❧

When food disappoints you

When Sally peeked into the break room one morning at work, she noticed that someone had brought in a three-layer chocolate cake. All morning long she anticipated having a piece of it during her coffee break. But when she took the first bite, she realized the cake was dry and crumbly.

How disappointing! Sally had really looked forward to this treat, but now it didn't even taste very good. Just in case she was wrong, Sally took another bite, then another.

She kept hoping that the taste would get better, but of course, it didn't. After she finished eating the piece of cake, she felt even more disappointed because she hadn't experienced the flavor or the texture she'd wanted.

Match what you want

When you eat something in order to appreciate a flavor, make sure the food matches what you want. Think carefully about how you expect the food to taste. Evaluate all aspects of it, such as whether it's too cold or too hot. Decide if it's overly salty, too dry, or even too moist.

Food isn't always perfect. In fact, sometimes when your body needs fuel, you'll be faced with mediocre food and decide to eat it anyway.

But food will never magically change into your dream taste. If you're eating to appreciate flavors and a food doesn't taste as good as you'd hoped, stop eating it! Then get rid of the rest so you don't reach for it again to see if it got any better!

Let it go

If you aren't enjoying the taste of a food but you keep eating anyway, you may be slipping into a type of emotional eating. Perhaps you think that wanting your favorite food seems "bad," so you force yourself to eat something you don't like.

Maybe as a child you always had to finish what you put on your plate, whether you liked it or not. Let go of any old rules that say eat your food, even when it doesn't taste very good. *If you don't love it—leave it!*

TODAY

- Choose a favorite treat for this exercise. Take a small bite of food, then think about how it tastes. Is it good? Wonderful? Just fair? Is it the correct temperature or is it a little too warm or too cold?

- Take another bite and then decide whether or not this food meets your expectations. Is it truly awesome or do you feel disappointed with it?

- In your notebook, write down your response to the food you're eating. If you decide it's absolutely perfect, feel free to enjoy some more. But if you realize it's not tasting very good, stop! Don't keep hoping it'll get better—because it won't.

❧ DAY 27 ❧

Eat dessert when it's special

You've probably heard the line, "Life is short; eat dessert first." But often dessert is what pushes you over your calorie goals or makes you uncomfortably full. Maybe it's time for you to get more particular about desserts.

You can certainly manage desserts by using your skills such as savoring, eating reasonable serving sizes, and planning smaller amounts, less often. But because desserts can be so tempting, you may need a few more tricks to handle them.

To get control over sweets and desserts, consider making a policy that you will eat dessert only when it's *special*. This label includes not just the food itself, but also the setting and the people you're with.

Is this the one?

Suppose your sister invites you to a birthday party where she serves homemade carrot cake. This occasion is special because you love your family and enjoy being with them. Plus, your sister makes the best carrot cake in the world. So in this case you label the carrot cake as "special" because it includes the right setting, great people, and excellent food.

Now picture yourself attending an all-day seminar at a large hotel. For dessert you are offered a huge piece of carrot cake. It looks wonderful, but you hesitate. First, this carrot cake is probably not unique or the best one you'll ever eat. Also, you're in a very ordinary setting, sharing lunch with people you may never see again. This time you decide to skip the cake because it doesn't fit the category of special.

Determine what's special

Think about your favorite desserts and then decide which ones are truly special and which ones are ordinary. Would you pick the chocolate suicide layer cake at your neighborhood restaurant? Or would you hold out for your mom's apple pie or the brownies you make when the grandkids visit?

Don't try to justify eating dessert by saying, "But they're all special." No, they're not! Realistically, you know that a lot of desserts aren't all that wonderful.

So pick the ones you truly do love and then get even more specific by deciding exactly which type you like best. For example, if you love cheesecake, do you want one that's smooth? Heavy? Dense? Topped with strawberries? Or do you prefer one flavored with caramel and nuts? When you evaluate desserts or sweets, become selective and eat only the ones that match your ideal flavor.

TODAY

- Make a list of desserts that you want to include on your *special* list.

- Think carefully about the taste and texture each one should have. For each of your dream desserts, write a few words to describe it.

- Add a list of situations that are special enough to justify eating dessert.

❧ DAY 28 ❧

Eating because it's there

As you walk past your friend's desk at work, you grab a handful of corn chips and munch away. You do the same thing with doughnuts at the bank or the free samples at the grocery store. During an afternoon meeting, you eat cookies along with everyone else. Later, you join your friends for a popcorn and soda break.

In all of these situations, you probably weren't hungry. You also weren't having any big psychological needs. You simply ate because the food was *there*.

When you grab food because it's in front of you, you're not trying to appreciate flavors. In fact, most likely you already know how the food will taste, and often you don't even pay much attention to it.

Stop automatic eating

To stop this autopilot eating, tell yourself this magic line:

I don't eat food just because it's there.

Then catch yourself during those times when you reach for food simply because it came into your line of vision.

To use this concept effectively, you have to be willing to let food opportunities pass you by. Just because someone brings doughnuts to a staff meeting or serves cookies at a gathering doesn't mean you have to eat them.

The same is true of chips or appetizers at a happy-hour

party. Remind yourself that you don't have to eat those foods just because they happen to be there.

Ignore food

Learn how to ignore food instead of chasing it. For example, practice walking past the doughnut box or the grocery-store samples without taking even a small taste. Do the same thing with hot dogs at the hardware store, popcorn at work, and the dish of candy on your mom's end table. Even if it looks good, skip eating food that simply shows up in front of you.

Anytime you're around tempting food, remind yourself that you eat for two reasons: to fuel your body or to appreciate flavors. But you do *not* eat just because the food is there. You'll be amazed how much your eating patterns will improve as a result of using this simple rule.

TODAY

- In your journal, write the phrase, "I don't eat food just because it's there." Then write the same words on sticky notes and post them any place you need reminders.

- Memorize this phrase, focus on it, and integrate it into your day.

- When tempting snacks show up unexpectedly, quickly remind yourself of your policy, and then walk away from the food.

☘ DAY 29 ☘

Handheld foods

It starts innocently enough. You reach for a few potato chips or a handful of nuts. Maybe you open a bag of M&M's. As soon as the first handful is gone, you reach for another one. The next thing you know, you get caught in a hand-to-mouth pattern that's almost impossible to stop.

Think about all the foods that come in bite-sized servings or ones that you eat from your hand. Some of the most common handheld foods include cheese, crackers, chips, cookies, and nuts, as well as small-sized candies such as M&M's.

You can also get into trouble with appetizers and party snacks. All of these can quickly become magnets, drawing you back to them again and again.

Addictive snack foods

Snacks aren't really bad food. They just have a sneaky ability to hook you into overeating without realizing it. To be able to enjoy your handheld snacks without becoming addicted to them, you need to set up strategies that will keep those foods in the bowl instead of in your hand.

Start by putting a buffer between any bite-sized foods and your mouth. When you eat a snack, transfer your serving amount from the original container to a plate or a bowl.

For example, place one cupful of popcorn into a cereal bowl. When you finish eating it, decide if you want to fill the bowl again. By putting your food into a serving dish, you'll have to stop and think each time before you refill it.

Use a fork

Here's another trick that will change the way you manage handheld foods. Any time you eat one of these small-sized foods, consider using a utensil. For example, try eating M&M's with a fork. Slide nuts into a spoon before tossing them into your mouth. Pour a stack of tortilla chips or other small snacks on a plate, and then cut them into pieces before you nibble them.

After a while you'll realize this feels pretty silly. And you'll probably eat less because the reward doesn't seem worth the effort it takes to put the food into a spoon.

TODAY

- Select a handheld food item such as nuts, chips, or candy pieces. Measure out a precise serving such as one-fourth cup or two tablespoons and then put this amount on a plate.

- Sit down at a table with the food in front of you. Using a fork or a spoon, eat one piece at a time. Notice how it feels to eat your snack this way.

- In your journal, write a few notes about how you will manage handheld foods in the future.

☙ DAY 30 ☙
Postpone eating

Once you start eating snack foods, it can be really hard to stop. Maybe you believe the advertising line, "You can't eat just one." With appetizers, snack-type foods, and even cookies or desserts, both the taste and the texture trick your mouth into wanting more.

To change the way you manage these foods, decide that you will *postpone eating* them. Tell yourself you can always have some of the food, but that you'll wait awhile before taking the first taste. Sometimes you'll wait ten minutes; other times you might hold off for a couple of hours.

Remind yourself to wait

Picture a card party or other social gathering where there are snack bowls of honey-roasted cashews, almond bark, and chocolate-covered pretzels sitting right at your elbow.

When you first arrive, look carefully at all the great-looking snacks or other foods. But don't eat *anything* until the very end of the event. Anytime you're tempted to give in and start nibbling, just remind yourself you can eat anything you want, but you'll wait until later.

When the games are finished and it's almost time to go home, decide if you still want some of the snacks. If you do, go ahead and eat them.

But at this point, you'll only have time for one or two pieces instead of half a pound. And by not eating until the last ten minutes of the gathering, you'll do a lot less damage than if you had nibbled all evening.

Minimize the amount

This system will also help you pace yourself at restaurants. Just *postpone* eating the foods that arrive early. Instead of reaching into the bread basket or the bowl of tortilla chips, promise yourself that you'll have some, but you'll hold off for a while.

When your meal arrives, go ahead and add one roll or a few of the chips to your plate. This way you still get to enjoy the flavor, but you prevent yourself from gobbling down several rolls or an entire bowl of chips.

This technique also works great for avoiding taking seconds or eating dessert. Assure yourself the fun is still coming and you can always have the food if you want it. Then postpone eating it until the very last minute, right before people leave the table or pay the bill. By then you'll only have time to eat a small amount. You might even decide you no longer want any and you'll skip the extra calories.

TODAY

- Watch for places where you can postpone eating. Hold off as long as possible, especially with snack foods or sweets.

- Record each of the foods you postponed and then note how much you ate compared to your usual amount.

- Notice whether by postponing eating, you're able to skip some foods entirely.

DAYS 21–30 COMPLETED!

You've come this far in your 100 days . . .

Don't stop now. If you're struggling to stick with it, push yourself to finish *one more day.* You'll immediately be another day closer to achieving your weight-loss goals.

Just do one more day!

❧ DAYS 31-40 ❧

LISTEN TO YOUR BODY

DAY 31   Hunger scale

DAY 32   The five-hour rule

DAY 33   Fullness scale

DAY 34   Listen accurately

DAY 35   The eating pause

DAY 36   Slow down your eating

DAY 37   I love to eat!

DAY 38   Food as power

DAY 39   Flavor or texture?

DAY 40   Having an eating experience

❧ DAY 31 ❧

Hunger scale

How do you decide when you're hungry? Do you watch the clock and eat at predetermined times, or do you tend to wait until you get hunger signals?

When it's time to eat, most people will start to notice physical cues such as a growling stomach, fatigue, or a slight headache. But if you typically nibble all day, grab food on the run, or regularly eat for emotional reasons, you may stop noticing these signals. Eventually you can even lose touch with your normal intuitive ability to recognize hunger.

The three-point hunger scale

Here's a simple way to fine-tune your hunger awareness. Using the three-point scale below, think about your body's signals for hunger or the need for food. Consider zero on the scale as being neutral—the place where you're not hungry and not full. This might be an hour or two after eating.

HUNGER LEVELS

0	Neutral, not hungry, not full
−1	A *little* hungry
−2	*Very* hungry
−3	*Starved, way too* hungry

At the first sign of a *little* hunger, you reach a *minus one* on the scale. Perhaps you feel hollow or your stomach growls, making you realize it's lunchtime. If you're quite busy or preoccupied, you might ignore these sensations and quickly forget about them.

Then an hour or two later, you suddenly realize that you're *very* hungry. You're now at a *minus two* on the scale. If you still don't eat, eventually you'll reach the point where you feel *starved*. When you're way too hungry and ready to eat everything in sight, you're at a *minus three* on the scale.

Catch it right away

To manage hunger effectively, you need to recognize it and respond to it when you're at a *minus one* on the hunger scale. As soon as you feel the first twinge or awareness of hunger, make note that it's time for food. Then plan to eat soon or at least within the next 20 to 30 minutes.

Of course, you can't always drop everything and run for food at the first hunger pang. But don't ignore your hunger signals. If necessary, plan ahead so that when your body speaks and tells you it's time to eat, you've got food readily available.

TODAY

- Start watching for hunger signals such as having a growling stomach, fatigue, headache, or loss of focus. Notice if you feel somewhat weak or shaky, grouchy, listless, or faint.

- In your notebook, write down the sensations you felt. Describe how you knew you were hungry.

- Whenever you recognize a hunger signal, respond to it and eat something within 20 to 30 minutes.

❧ DAY 32 ❧
The five-hour rule

Here's an interesting question. If you're *really* hungry, do you need more food than if you're just a *little* hungry? As a rule, the answer is no—you just think you do. When you feel "starved," you're more likely to overeat, even though your body would be satisfied with a lot less food.

Brenda is a sales representative who pitches her products to executives. When she's meeting with people at dinner, she usually doesn't eat much during the main part of the day so that she can have more food in the evening.

By the time she sits down for her meal, Brenda feels starved. Because she's become so hungry, she eats a lot of appetizers and snacks, then consumes a large dinner as well. By letting herself become way too hungry, Brenda loses her ability to judge portion amounts.

Eat every three to five hours

For most people, getting too hungry simply contributes to more eating problems. When you feel really famished, you're a lot more likely to eat too much. You're also far less particular about your food choices.

To prevent this, use a *five-hour rule* to manage your hunger. Anytime you go longer than five hours between eating, you greatly increase the risk of overeating.

In his book *The 3-Hour Diet*, weight-loss coach Jorge Cruise suggests that dieters space all their meals and snacks exactly three hours apart. Based on research on how food intake affects metabolism, Jorge believes this interval gives you the best level of energy at the same time it helps your body manage your weight more effectively.

To protect yourself from getting too hungry, maintain a stash of healthy snacks that you can grab quickly. Carry your food along when you go shopping, travel on airplanes, or attend long meetings at work. Don't worry about looking foolish. People will perceive you as someone who really cares about healthy eating.

Use both hunger and the clock

Sometimes hunger alone doesn't provide you with an adequate signal for when to eat. If you tend to go way too long between fuel stops, or you never get hunger signals, you may need a different approach.

In this case, use a combination of both tools—listening to your body *and* watching the clock. Plan to set up mealtimes in advance, and then regardless of your hunger level, eat within 30 minutes of your designated time.

TODAY

- Plan your mealtimes carefully, aiming for no more than three to five hours between meals or snacks.

- Write your plan in your notebook, and then record the times you eat.

- Notice any patterns, such as whether you tend to overeat when you go too long between meals.

☀ DAY 33 ☀

Fullness scale

Now you know how to recognize hunger. But how do you know when you're full or you've eaten enough? Unlike what you might think, to recognize fullness, you have to listen to your stomach instead of looking at your plate.

As you are eating, your stomach muscles begin to expand in order to accommodate the food. By paying careful attention to how your abdominal area feels, you can determine the precise amount of food your body requires.

The three-point fullness scale

To recognize fullness, you can use a three-point scale similar to the one for levels of hunger. Remember that zero on the eating scale is neutral—you're not hungry, not full. Usually you're at this level about midway between meals, when food isn't on your mind at all.

FULLNESS LEVELS	
0	*Neutral,* not hungry, not full
+1	*Satisfied,* comfortable, just right
+2	*Too full,* a little uncomfortable
+3	*Stuffed,* miserable

The next time you're enjoying a meal, pay close attention to how you feel as you're eating. At some point you'll begin to notice a slight pressure or change within your stomach area.

Soon after that, you'll reach a level where you feel satisfied and your abdomen feels comfortable or *just right*. You've now reached a *plus one* on the fullness scale.

Suppose you really like your food, so you keep eating. Before long, you'll notice your abdomen starts to feel slightly puffy and you'll realize you're too full. This equals a *plus two* on the scale. Sometimes you'll notice this level after just one extra bite; other times it will take an extra serving of food. But either way, you'll still be too full.

Now picture eating a holiday meal such as the kind you might have on Thanksgiving Day. Because you love the special foods, you keep eating long after you're already full. At some point, you'll realize you feel stuffed, almost miserable. That's when you reach a *plus three* on the fullness scale.

Work at being able to recognize when you reach a *plus one* or the exact spot where you feel totally *satisfied* or *just right*. Then regardless of what's left on your plate, stop eating right at that point.

TODAY

- Next time you eat a meal or snack, place your hand on your abdomen and monitor how your stomach feels.

- Notice when you feel comfortable or satisfied, the exact level of *plus one*. When you reach that point, stop and look at the amount you've eaten.

- Write down how much food you ate, and then add a few notes on how it feels to be satisfied, not full. Practice this skill until you can recognize the *plus one* level at nearly every meal.

❦ DAY 34 ❦
Listen accurately

To recognize the exact moment when you've eaten enough food, you have to pay close attention to your body. Watch carefully for the first signs of feeling comfortable or just right. The moment you begin thinking you may be at that point, ask yourself: "Does my stomach feel satisfied? Do I feel like I've had enough food?" Nearly always, the answer is yes.

Your stomach, not your head

The fullness scale is not the same as the 20-minute signal to your brain, indicating you've reached satiety. Instead, you learn how to monitor fullness by listening to the source—the abdominal muscles that cover the stomach.

Think about this—when you feel way too full, you hold your stomach, not your head. So by noticing the way your stomach feels, not what your head thinks, you'll be able to recognize the early signs that indicate you're feeling satisfied.

When full feels good

What if you enjoy the sensation of being full? Maybe you've connected feeling *stuffed* with also feeling powerful, nurtured, or safe. Perhaps large family meals always helped you feel connected to others. If so, you might still relate feeling full to memories of happy times and good food.

If you realize that you *like* feeling stuffed, you may need to work on changing your belief that full is a good sensation. You

might even want to start thinking of stuffed as being a distaste-
ful, obnoxious feeling rather than a desired one.

Instead of enjoying the sensation of being overly full, begin
labeling it as *uncomfortable*. Make a conscious decision that you
no longer want to feel that way and that instead, you want to
feel *comfortable* or *satisfied*.

If you've been overeating for many years, it may take some
time to adjust to the goal of never letting yourself get way too
full. But eventually you can learn to appreciate having a healthy,
positive body that doesn't want to feel stuffed.

TODAY

- Eat a meal or snack but stop right at the point of feeling
  comfortable or a *plus one* on the scale.

- In your journal, describe how this level feels to you. Recall
  times in the past when you've eaten until you felt stuffed.
  Write a note describing that and then compare the two
  feelings.

- Think about what it means to feel full or stuffed. Is it comforting or nurturing? Does having a full belly make you
  feel stronger or more confident? Are you getting away
  with something you couldn't do as a child? Record your
  insights.

☘ DAY 35 ☘

The eating pause

During my years of weight-loss counseling, I discovered a fascinating behavior that helps people know when they are full. At some point in the process of eating a meal, most people stop briefly and lay down their forks or put down the food they're holding in their hands. Then they might stretch, talk a little, watch TV, or even read the newspaper.

After this *pause* in their eating, people will often glance down at their food and decide they want more. Maybe they think it still looks good or they just want more of the taste in their mouths, so they pick up their forks and resume eating. But after finishing the rest of their food, they exclaim, "I shouldn't have eaten that because now I'm too full!"

Stopping at the "pause"

When you naturally pause in your eating, you're usually at the exact point where you feel *satisfied* or *comfortable*. In fact, this pause seems to correlate exactly with the moment your stomach indicates it's taken in enough food. If you continue to eat, you quickly move to the level of being *too full*.

Each person responds differently to the eating pause. Some people push their plates aside, subconsciously concluding they've had enough. Others wait a few minutes and then begin eating again. In this case, they miss the signal to stop.

Watch carefully for the eating pause, and then use it as a guide to stop eating. If you typically ignore it and eat more, you risk gaining weight because you'll always tend to take in more calories than your body needs.

Built-in signal

As a weight-loss tool, you can use the eating pause anywhere. It works especially well for times when you can't choose your portion amounts, such as at restaurants or banquets. Build the habit of watching for this internal sign that tells you when to stop eating.

Even when you're just having a snack, letting your food sit for a while usually indicates you don't need to eat any more. Once you're able to consistently recognize the eating pause, you'll always be able to tell how much food your body needs.

Start watching other people eat, especially when you're at dinners or in restaurants. You'll be amazed at how easily you can spot others taking an eating pause. You'll also notice that many people pause but keep eating anyway.

TODAY

- At each meal and snack, notice when you pause in your eating. In your notebook, record how you recognized the pause as well as how much you had eaten at that point.

- After you've paused, stop eating, regardless of the amount you have left. Wait for at least two hours before eating again.

- If you realize you were still hungry after the pause, work at fine-tuning your listening skills and improving your ability to use the eating pause as a tool.

❦ DAY 36 ❦

Slow down your eating

The eating pause provides a very distinct cue for knowing when you should stop eating. But sometimes the pause will irritate you because you still want the rest of your food.

Nancy said, "As I looked at all the lasagna left on my plate, I thought, 'No! That can't possibly be right. Surely my body needs more than this.' But I knew I had paused, so I stopped eating anyway. As the minutes passed, I knew the pause had been right and I was finished."

Practice your listening skills

You may not realize it, but your body's needs for fuel aren't always consistent. Some days you need more food than others. If you feel hungry, you probably do need to eat. But strong hunger signals don't always mean you need *a lot* of food. By listening to your body, you should be able to tell exactly how much fuel you need at any given time.

If you stop eating in response to the pause, but then you feel hungry a couple of hours later, it doesn't mean you didn't read the signals right. Instead, your body simply wants food again and it's letting you know that it's time.

As with any skill, listening to your body requires practice. Just when you think you've become adept at recognizing the *satisfied* point, one day you'll misjudge it and eat to the level of *too full*. But don't give up. The longer you use these skills, the more they will become second nature, giving you a solid method for knowing what your body needs.

Slow down and listen

To recognize your body signals, you may have to slow down your pace. If you're like a lot of people, you probably eat quickly much of the time. But when you eat too quickly, you can slip right past the eating pause and become too full before you realize it.

Here's an easy way to train yourself to eat more slowly. At the start of your meal, set a timer or the alarm on your watch for *20 minutes*. Then pace yourself (even if you're just eating a sandwich) so that you'll be finishing the last bite of your food when the time is up. Eventually you will become more conscious of eating slowly and you'll learn to pace yourself automatically.

TODAY

- With at least one of your meals today, set a timer and pace your eating to make the meal last for at least 20 minutes.

- Make a game out of catching other people doing the eating pause with their food, then ask them, "Are you feeling satisfied and comfortable right now? Do you feel like you've had enough food?"

- Teach the eating pause concept to several people. In your notebook, record their responses to using this technique.

❧ DAY 37 ❧

I love to eat!

Do you love to eat? If you're like a lot of people, you love to cook, love to share food with others, and just plain like food! Perhaps you tend to wolf down your favorite meals and then reach for seconds because the food is so good. Maybe after finishing a huge meal, you roll away from the table feeling stuffed but satisfied because you simply loved eating.

First of all, it's perfectly okay to love eating and to appreciate good food. But you need to recognize there's a big difference between appreciating the *flavors* of your food and liking the way you *feel* as you eat it. When you say you love to eat, you may simply be providing an excuse for using food to appease some of your emotional needs.

What do you really love?

Think about what you love about food. Are you sure that it's the flavor and the aroma? Or is it possible that you enjoy the sensations of eating more than the food itself?

When you chomp down on a huge steak or you tackle a giant plate of spaghetti, what do you notice most? Are you hooked on the taste, or are you delighting more in the texture of the food? Perhaps you enjoy swallowing and you like the way the bites feel as they slide down your throat.

It's possible that it's not the food that you love. Instead, maybe you crave experiences around food, such as eating while you're watching sports on TV. Or when life feels unhappy or

80

difficult, you can make your problems fade away by eating, drinking, and laughing along with other people.

Are there particular times of day when you love to eat? Have you ever noticed whether you love food more during the evening than in the early morning? If so, you might be using food to meet an emotional need, such as a reward at the end of the day.

Appreciate food

You don't have to stop "loving to eat." Just make sure you take time to appreciate the flavors and textures of what you love. Remember to savor your meals and to pay special attention to the first two bites of any food. Decide whether some of your favorite desserts are truly special or if they're just ordinary, and that sometimes you could skip them.

TODAY

- Make a list of foods you absolutely love.

- Explore what you love about these foods. Consider the flavor and texture as well as the settings where you typically eat them.

- In addition to the flavors of good food, notice other things that you love about eating. Is it possible that what you love isn't related to the food at all? Record your insights in your notebook.

❧ DAY 38 ❧

Food as power

Suppose two executives meet in a restaurant where they plan to negotiate a business deal. Each of them orders a plate of food, and then they eat while they discuss their plans. Usually the person who dominates the conversation is not the one on a diet.

In this setting, food relates to a perception of power. With business meals as well as many stressful situations that involve food, eating can become linked to your need to feel stronger or have more power in life.

Conquering food

You may have discovered that sometimes food helps you feel more important or confident. When you eat a huge amount of food, you may get a feeling of accomplishment or even a sense of "conquering" the meal.

For example, after you finish off a dozen doughnuts, a huge steak, or a large plate of spaghetti, something inside you might think, "See, I can do something in my life." It's almost as though food is the enemy and you just beat it!

In the same way, if you feel powerless in other areas of your life, food can provide a way to overcome feelings of insecurity. This certainly doesn't mean that you can't love eating great food. In fact, by appreciating flavors, you can enjoy the most wonderful food in the world.

But look carefully at what food and eating does for you. Maybe at times you don't even notice the taste of food at all.

Instead, "loving to eat" simply gives you a sense of power in your life.

Food makes you feel strong

Maybe you've developed the habit of reaching for food when you feel insecure. Or you eat to pump up your courage before meeting with your boss or making a challenging presentation. Many people admit that during times when they feel stressed or anxious, they *eat to feel strong*.

It's easy to let food fill the emotional holes in your life so you don't have to face them. If you're feeling uneasy or you want to boost your self-esteem, food will usually provide an easy solution.

Learn to recognize times when you're tempted to eat to feel strong. Instead of justifying it by saying "I love to eat," tackle the real issue and try to figure out how to become stronger emotionally—without reaching for food.

TODAY

- Think about situations or places in life where you feel that you do have power, as well as ones where you don't. Make a list of each of these.

- Write down several ideas for how you can feel powerful without using food to meet this need.

- Do something today that makes you feel strong and powerful as a person.

❊ DAY 39 ❊

Flavor or texture?

Do you like sweets and desserts or do you tend to reach for salty foods such as potato chips? Would you rather eat a crunchy oatmeal cookie or a gooey caramel roll? Do you love the pungent flavor of blue cheese dressing? Or might you favor the zing of a spicy burrito or a bowl of green chili?

Each of your answers reveals another aspect of what you love about food. Often it's not the flavor but the *texture* of foods that keeps you reaching for more. When you can't seem to stop eating a favorite food, it's possible you simply love how it feels in your mouth.

Flavor may not matter

As you pay attention to the foods you love, you may discover many of them appeal to you only because of their texture. In fact, some foods don't have much flavor at all, but their texture keeps you coming back for more.

Think about which types of food textures you enjoy most. Do you tend to prefer crunchy and chewy or soft and smooth? What about harsh, slippery, or tingly? Consider the *mouth feel* of the foods you like best. When you bite into a thick, juicy cheeseburger, what sensations do you get with that first bite?

Mentally feel the contrast between eating a strip of beef jerky and an ice-cream cone. Picture eating cashews, and then switch to peanut butter. What do you think makes the difference in why specific textures appeal to you? You may discover your "love" of some foods is based entirely on the way they feel in your mouth.

Emotions behind the textures

When you begin eating something and you can't seem to stop, think about what the texture might be doing for you. Does it give you a way to chew hard and fast, the way you'd like to "chew on" your boss? Maybe it feels soothing or comforting, causing you to eat more so you can feel these emotions again and again.

If you recognize you're eating for texture, try to identify what you might need emotionally. After you figure this out, address those needs in some other way instead of using food to take care of them.

TODAY

- Pay special attention to both the flavor and texture of each of the foods you eat today.

- Select one of your favorite foods. In your journal, describe its texture. Use creative words as if you were writing a gourmet review for a magazine.

- See if you can correlate your favorite textures with specific events, people, or emotional needs. Plan how you can handle these in other ways.

☘ DAY 40 ☘

Having an eating experience

Many times the joy of eating isn't about food as much as it's about our social events or family get-togethers. During these gatherings, you may find you get caught up in the *experience of eating* because it's part of the fun of being with others.

But by separating the qualities and tastes of your food away from the situation you're eating it in, you can learn to manage the amounts you eat much differently.

Notice the tastes

Sometimes we don't want food at all. Instead, we simply want to enjoy being around it. Shopping for food, then cooking it and arranging it can bring us great delight. In other words, we want an *experience* around food.

Instead of proclaiming that you love all food, look for ways you can have eating experiences. Imagine you're a famous chef sampling your latest creations. Or pretend you're a food spy and ask things such as, "Does this cookie contain cinnamon or is nutmeg providing that flavor edge?"

When you're cooking, make an effort to appreciate the taste of new spices such as basil or coriander. Evaluate the flavors, the seasoning, and the temperature of every food, and then answer the question: "Is it perfect yet?"

Dig more deeply into your love of food and eating. Do you ever get caught up in the social aspects of eating, then simply let food blend into the total event? In fact, when does enjoying a flavor or texture change into an eating experience?

Create your own eating experience

You can create an atmosphere that meets your needs without depending on food to make an event enjoyable. To do this, intentionally plan to have an eating experience.

When you recognize your goal is to enjoy a meal, consider setting things up to make this happen. Let the food become a minor part of your event, perhaps even choosing a simple meal of soup or salad for your experience. If you decide to go to a restaurant for this exercise, select one based on the type of experience you want to have.

Think about what you really want from this eating event. Are you in the mood for a quiet, romantic evening? Or do you crave the energy from places with loud music and a constant conversational buzz? If you prefer quiet, create an eating experience at home by arranging the room, decorating the table, and choosing music that will add to your event.

TODAY

- Recall some of your most enjoyable eating experiences. What made these times so special?

- In your journal, describe one or two of your favorite types of eating experiences.

- Using this description, plan an eating experience that matches your needs. After you finish the meal, record your favorite details from it.

DAYS 31–40 COMPLETED!

You've come this far in your 100 days . . .

Don't stop now. If you're struggling to stick with it, push yourself to finish *one more day.* You'll immediately be another day closer to achieving your weight-loss goals.

Just do one more day!

❧ DAYS 41–50 ❧

JUMP-START MOTIVATION

☙ DAY 41 ❧
Motivation is a choice

I just can't seem to get myself motivated! Do these words sound familiar? Even the most dedicated dieters will sometimes feel at a loss as to how to get going.

Motivation affects everything! From staying on your diet to cleaning your house, it provides the power behind all of your actions and helps you follow through with good intentions. Motivation becomes the push that helps you get things done.

When motivation is strong, you might not even realize it or give it much thought. But when it goes away, you're usually in big trouble! Often you won't have any idea where it went or how to get it back.

Unfortunately, your motivation doesn't drop out of the sky or suddenly reappear after an absence. You can't open the junk drawer and shout, "Look! I just found my motivation!" Every once in a while, you just need a way to jump-start your actions as well as keep yourself moving once you get started.

Create it yourself

Although it may seem as if it simply pops up unexpectedly, motivation is actually a *choice*. You create it yourself through your thoughts, your self-talk, and your attitude. Even when you don't have a shred of energy, you can still access your motivation if you want to.

Because your drive and energy originate inside your head, you have the ability to motivate yourself anytime you want. You just have to get up out of your chair and make it happen.

Invent new tricks

Instead of waiting for inspiration to hit, you can learn how to build it yourself. To do this, you have to invent new tricks and create fresh ideas that will inspire you toward action.

Pick an area you'd like to change and then make a list of every possible action you could take that would move you toward that desired goal. For example, to get your exercise program back on track, your list might include:

- Set my alarm earlier.

- Lay out my exercise clothes.

- Put a water bottle in the refrigerator.

- Buy a new CD of energizing music.

Then simply do the things on your list and surprise—you'll have boosted your motivation! You may still have to push yourself during times when you don't feel like doing your exercise. But if you know how to get yourself started, you'll always be able to make progress.

TODAY

- In your notebook, write the words "Motivation is a choice." Focus on accepting and believing this.

- Write down a few tricks and ideas that have helped boost your motivation in the past.

- Do at least one of these today. For example, you might set your exercise shoes in front of the door to help motivate you to take your walk.

❧ DAY 42 ❧

Make it matter

Do you ever get discouraged and wonder if you really care about your weight or your fitness level? Anytime you sit on the fence regarding staying on your diet or exercise program, you'll almost always fall to the wrong side.

Ambivalence is one of the biggest enemies of change. If you aren't sure that you really want to take action on something such as your weight, ambivalence will usually win. To get past this roadblock, you have to raise the importance of your goal and *make it matter.*

When something becomes really important to you, getting motivated is easy. You simply jump into action, not stopping to think about what's involved. For example, if your mother calls to say that she's coming for a visit, you suddenly become motivated to clean the house. Instantly the dishes in the sink and the towels on the floor become more critical.

How does your weight affect you?

In the same way, you can boost your motivation to stay on a diet plan by making the outcome more important. To do this, think about all the things that bother you about being overweight, and then convince yourself that it's crucial you make changes in this area.

Now make a list of all the ways your weight affects your life. For example, is it hurting your health or your energy? Maybe it's harming your self-esteem. Does it influence the ways you cope with emotions or manage stress? Do you wish you could wear nicer clothes or at least fit into the ones in your closet?

Raise the importance

On a scale of 1 to 10, rate each of these issues based on how much they bother you or affect your life.

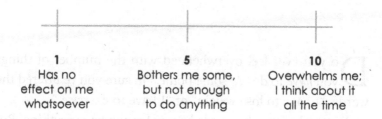

1	5	10
Has no effect on me whatsoever	Bothers me some, but not enough to do anything	Overwhelms me; I think about it all the time

Now push the numbers higher by making the outcomes more important. For example, if you rated having more energy or wearing your favorite jeans as a 4 on the scale, tell yourself that *not* having these goals affects you a lot more than that.

Convince yourself that these issues are so important that you *must* see changes in them. Then push their importance to a 7 or an 8 on the scale. *Make them matter* by focusing on how much you'd like to see improvement.

TODAY

- Make a list of ways that being overweight bothers you. Using the scale of 1 to 10, rate each of these issues based on how much it affects you.

- Now raise the importance of each one of them and mentally push the level even higher.

- Remind yourself that your weight bothers you *a lot* and you can't wait to see improvement.

❧ DAY 43 ❧

Choose to, not have to

Do you ever feel overwhelmed with the number of things you *have* to do? At some point, I'm sure you've uttered the words, "I have to lose weight" or "I have to exercise."

We tend to use the words *have to* for almost everything. But in reality, most of us don't like being told that we *have to* do things. In fact, sometimes that little *have to* phrase can make us rebel and do the opposite. It's as though the child inside reacts by saying, "Oh yeah? Just try and make me!"

Change your words

The real truth is you don't *have to* do anything. This includes going to work, cleaning the house, or even feeding the dog. You choose to do these things because you don't like what might happen if you don't do them.

Maybe you're protesting, "You don't understand! I really do have to lose weight." Guess what? Telling yourself "I have to" didn't work last year, and it won't change your behavior now either. So stop saying it.

Starting today, instead of saying "I have to" when discussing your actions or goals, substitute the words *"I choose to."* Now the phrase "I have to go to work" becomes "I choose to go to work." And "I have to lose weight" becomes "I choose to lose weight."

Saying "I choose to" puts you in charge and affirms that you want to see results. For example, you choose to stick with your diet because you want certain outcomes such as feeling better or fitting into the clothes hanging in your closet.

Choose your actions

To help you see the difference in saying the words "choose to," read each of the following phrases twice. The first time use the words "I have to . . ." and then the second time replace them with "I choose to . . ."

I *have* to (versus I *choose* to) . . . go to work.

. . . stay on my diet plan.

. . . stop yelling at my kids.

. . . clean my house.

. . . exercise today.

You can't force yourself to lose weight or to stay on a diet by saying "I have to." So start eliminating the harsh, parental self-talk that makes you feel oppressed or rebellious. Anytime you feel as if you *have to* do something, say *"I choose to,"* and then take steps that move you toward the outcomes you want.

TODAY

- Start catching times when you say, "I have to . . ." Regardless of the issue you're facing, switch your words and say, "I choose to . . ."

- Train yourself to use this phrase more regularly by saying things such as, "I choose to get up early for my meeting" or "I choose to sit here at my desk and type this report."

- Using the words "I choose to . . ." in your notebook, write a list of things you want to accomplish.

✿ DAY 44 ✿
It's not the right time

When you struggle with staying on your diet, it's easy to excuse your bad behavior by deciding that it simply wasn't *the right time*. You may be right. Sometimes it really isn't the right time to be on a diet. But since life will always include job challenges, dinner parties, and vacations, there will never be a perfect time to work on losing weight.

Evaluate your timing

If you're debating whether or not it's the right time to be on a weight-loss program, let these questions help you decide:

- Are you currently facing a *major life issue?* For example, are you getting a divorce, moving to a new home, or even finishing a degree? Issues of this magnitude usually happen only a dozen or so times in life, and when they do, it's truly not the right time to be on a diet.

- Is something in life demanding a huge amount of your *time and energy* right now? Things such as remodeling your home, planning your daughter's wedding, or even being a schoolteacher at the end of the year can all take a lot out of you. Dieting also requires a certain amount of energy, so if you're already feeling drained, you might need to hold off on your plan for a while.

- Are you simply dealing with your *ordinary life?* Just because your days are crammed with events, demands at work, and small children doesn't necessarily mean it's not the right time to lose weight.

In reality, you can make any time be the right time. Simply choose a time period that looks fairly reasonable and label it *the right time*. Then move past your excuses and make it work. Tell yourself that you are capable of eating right and exercising in spite of your hectic life. Then find a way to do it.

Is it really important?

If you keep going off a diet because it's not "the right time," maybe what you're really saying is that losing weight isn't important to you, at least not right now. That's okay. There's nothing wrong with moving it lower on your priority list.

But don't assume you can keep it there just because you're busy. When losing weight becomes important enough, you'll figure out how to make room for it being *the right time*.

TODAY

- Evaluate how your program is going so far. Is this a right time for you to work on losing weight?

- If not, make a list of reasons why it doesn't seem to be the right time. Measure your list against the criteria of major life events or any big issues that demand your time and energy.

- If losing weight is truly important to you, *make it the right time*. In your notebook, write a few ideas on how to get around the roadblocks in your daily life and make your diet work in spite of those obstacles.

※ DAY 45 ※

Food—important or not?

During the course of a day, how much do you think about food? A little? A lot? Most of the time? Do you finish one meal and immediately start planning what you'll eat next? What if you could eliminate food as the center of your life? You can—by choosing specific times to let food be *important,* and then other times, treating it as *unimportant.*

Is this important or not?

When you get into your car, you don't expect every trip to be inspiring or memorable. Sometimes you just need to go to the store or the post office.

In the same way, eating doesn't always have to be especially fun or exciting. Lots of times, food will be quite mundane, but since it's providing fuel, you have to eat it anyway. Instead of fretting about boring food, just label it as *unimportant.*

Now picture a vacation where you catch a beautiful sunset or discover a new road with breathtaking mountain scenery. On this kind of trip, your drive feels much more important.

When it comes to eating, a surprise birthday party or even an exotic new restaurant can suddenly change your view of food. During these times, you can make a decision to let food be *important.*

Just like the drive where you slow down and appreciate the scenery, you can do the same thing with food. Give it full attention and allow yourself to enjoy it. Appreciate the taste, enjoy the fun of the eating experience, and ask for the recipe.

Designating food as important doesn't give you permission to overeat. Instead, it allows you to openly appreciate and enjoy good food. If you've labeled food as important, make sure you don't punish yourself by saying things like, "I shouldn't be eating this!" Simply relax and enjoy it.

Pick and choose

Since you can't make food special all the time, be selective with when you call it important. Don't assume you have to give food special status just because it's part of an event. When you spend time with others, you can still choose to let food be unimportant and, instead, focus on giving love and attention to the people around you.

Rather than always making food the center of your day, be particular about how you view it. Simply choose when to make it *important* and when to let it be routine.

TODAY

- Think carefully about specific times you want to label food as important.

- In your notebook, make a list of times, places, or even specific foods that you would usually designate as *important*.

- With times or situations that aren't on your list, plan to view food as *unimportant*.

✿ DAY 46 ✿

If not food, then what?

After you decide to label more of your food as being *unimportant*, you may have to replace it with something else. Take out a piece of paper and write the numbers from 1 to 10 down the side of the page. Then write the word "food" in the first slot—number 1 on your list of important things.

Now come up with nine more items, including people, things, or events in life that are very important to you. You might add your kids, your job, or your health to the list.

Perhaps you'll include playing a favorite sport, going to the movies, or spending time with a good friend. Be as specific as possible with these items, even listing all the names of your children or your friends.

Make other things more important

After you have a total of 10 items, erase or scratch the word "food" off the number 1 spot. Then move it to the bottom of the list and label it as number 11. Next study your list and think about what else is really important in your life.

In the empty slot next to number 1, write a new item. You can choose a person or activity already on your list or add something new that you hadn't considered before.

Now review your list again and think about how you could give more attention to all of the non-food items that you labeled as important. Notice that when you lower the priority of food, you force yourself to put something else in its place as the dominant interest in your day.

Deepen commitment

In her delightful book *Passion*, author Barbara DeAngelis recommends selecting one area of life in which you'd like to feel more passion—perhaps your marriage, your job, or your emotional or spiritual growth.

She suggests that for one entire day, you simply deepen your commitment to this area, expressing this through your words and behavior. By the end of the day, you'll find you feel more passionate and committed to that person or issue.

As you focus on the non-food items on your list, look for ways you can give them more emphasis or attention. For example, you might spend time on the floor playing with your children. Or maybe you can plan a movie night or watch a favorite TV show with your spouse or a good friend. By increasing your commitment to these important things, you'll find you can replace food in your life more easily.

TODAY

- From the list you made earlier, write your new number 1 item on a piece of paper or sticky note.

- *Deepen your commitment* to this item. Spend time thinking, doing, or in some other way, focusing on this item, person, or activity. Assign it a very high priority, making it far more important than food.

- At the end of the day, write a few notes about how you now feel about this item or person. Over time, do this with the rest of your list.

❧ DAY 47 ❧
Kick the can't

I *can't* . . . These two little words will almost always keep you
from being successful. Think of all the situations where you
let these words slip out. For example,

- I can't stick with an exercise program.

- I can't resist my mom's desserts.

- I can't cook healthy meals.

Right after saying "I can't," you always provide some type of
legitimate excuse that justifies *why* you think it's true. For
example, with your weight-loss efforts, you can easily explain
why you *can't* eat right or exercise consistently.

Perhaps you believe it's not your fault you can't stay on a
diet. Maybe you blame lack of willpower or not having enough
time. You might even name a few people who don't support
you or who get in your way.

I'll find a way

Every time you tell yourself that you can't do something,
you cement it as truth. For example, when you say, "I can't stay
on a diet," you unconsciously make sure this statement is correct. Saying "I can't" is like tying a huge rock to your ankle, then
trying to run.

No matter how determined you are to reach your goals,
those "I can't" statements will nearly always keep you from

making progress. So starting today, banish the words "I can't" from your vocabulary! Instead, think about what's possible, then substitute the phrase, *"I'll find a way."*

Nothing is impossible

You can help this along by changing the way you talk about your efforts. Describe all your challenging goals as *"hard but not impossible."* Then whenever you think about your struggle, add the phrase, "I'll find a way."

For example, you might say, "It's hard but not impossible to avoid gaining my weight back, so I'll find a way." You might conclude the same thing about staying on a diet when you're visiting your family. It's hard but not impossible, so you just need to find a way.

Now add the phrase, *"Maybe I could . . ."* and then come up with a new action plan for each of these areas. For example, if you have trouble staying consistent with your exercise program, you might say, "It's hard to exercise regularly, but I'll find a way. Maybe I could start walking every day at lunchtime."

TODAY

- Write a list of things that you believe you *can't* do.

- Several times today, read through the list. With each item, say, "It's hard to _____ (fill in your "I can't"), but I'll find a way."

- For each item on the list, add the phrase, "Maybe I could . . ." and plan at least one action that will help you make progress.

❧ DAY 48 ❧

You gotta want to . . .

Even when you're very determined to change your attitude, sometimes you'll still feel there are certain things you can't do. But in reality, you might have a deeper reason for dragging your feet. Maybe deep down you don't really want to do the work or invest the time or effort it takes to change your life.

When you feel like you *can't* do something, stop and think about what you'd *really* like to say. For example, when you make the statement "I can't lose weight," you may really be saying, "I don't want to miss out on all the fun" or "I don't want to feel left out when everyone else is eating."

Of course, I want to!

If you're serious about making changes in your life, you may have to work on your *want to* skills. The next time you're tempted to say "I can't," substitute the words "I don't want to." You might confess, "I don't want to stay on a diet" or "I don't want to stop overeating when I visit my family."

Look back at the list of "I can't" items you wrote yesterday. Read them again, but instead of saying "I can't," change them to read *"I don't want to . . ."* Now the phrase "I can't exercise regularly" will become "I don't want to exercise regularly."

That certainly doesn't feel good, does it? Now, go through each of those "I can't" statements again, but this time start with the words, *"Wait a minute. Of course I want to!"* So now, your weak phrase "I can't exercise" would read, "Wait a minute. Of course I want to exercise regularly!"

Set tiny goals

If you still have a hard time taking action, split the issue apart and consider which pieces you don't feel ready to take on. For example, saying "I can't exercise" might mean you don't want to get hurt or feel exhausted.

Then set some tiny goals based on what you *can* do. Perhaps you can plan to walk for five or ten minutes a day or ride a bike for a few blocks at a time. You aren't as likely to reject these goals because you'll believe you can do them.

After you've determined your tiny steps, reinforce your new goals by saying, "Of course I want to . . . ." Then follow through with what you planned.

TODAY

- Go back to yesterday's list or even write a new list of goals or situations where you're inclined to say, "I can't."

- In front of each one, write the words, "Of course I want to . . ." reinforcing your plan to make it happen.

- Pick one of these goals and write it on a separate piece of paper along with the words, "Of course, I want to." Carry this with you and read it often.

❦ DAY 49 ❦
Just do something

You know what you want to accomplish and your goals are clear. Every day you tell yourself that you're ready to get started on your diet or exercise plan. But it doesn't happen. Days or even weeks go by and you still haven't done a thing. When you get into a rut that's so deep you can't see over the sides, you may feel as if you'll never get going again.

One step lights the fire

Here's an immediate solution for times when you can't seem to budge. Simply tell yourself

Just do something; then you're started.

Doing *something* moves you past the barrier of inertia. Then once you've started, your mind recognizes that you've been successful and it helps you keep going. All you need is one positive step—take one walk, eat one healthy meal, then mentally acknowledge that you're over the hump.

Getting started is critical to reviving motivation. That first step can be a killer, yet without it, you'll probably stay stuck. So the next time you feel immobilized, repeat the phrase "Just do something; then you're started" and put yourself back into action.

If you're trying to push a rock down a path, the hardest part is getting it to move. After it starts rolling, momentum takes over and keeps it going. The same concept is true with your eating or exercise efforts. After you've broken through your inertia, you need a way to keep going and build momentum.

Three days to success

With whatever step you've taken, plan to repeat it daily for a minimum of *three days*. Once you sustain a positive action for at least three days in a row, you'll begin to get back your confidence and regain a sense of control. And with a new attitude, you'll be more willing to stick with your plan.

The *just do something* concept will work for you again and again. Anytime your motivation slips away or you have a setback in your routine, just take *one step*. Get out of the rut, then stay with your efforts for three days and you'll find yourself back into a rhythm.

TODAY

- *Just do something*. Pick out the tiniest action you could take, whether it's to clean off one corner of your desk, eat a piece of fruit, or take a five-minute walk.

- Repeat this activity for each of the next two days and then celebrate the success of doing *something*.

- Make a list of your *just do something* ideas and record them in your notebook. During the next week, use one of them each day.

✵ DAY 50 ✵

10-minute solution

Now that you've actually done *something*, how will you keep yourself going? As you know, getting started is half the battle. But what if you don't feel like doing your activity again the next day? And how do you sustain your rhythm when the kids are crabby, the weather is bad, and your staff members all have the flu?

Something is better than nothing

To sustain your exercise plan, break it down into levels that you know you can handle. Then to get yourself going, use the concept of the *10-minute solution*.

Suppose you're trying to exercise every day. But at times you just don't feel like it and you can't seem to drag your feet out the door. Make a deal with yourself that says you only have to exercise for *10 minutes* and after that you can quit. Then go do it.

Sometimes at the end of 10 minutes, you'll feel relieved it's over and you'll stop. But other times you'll realize that you feel better and you might decide to keep going longer. Either way, you're a success!

Never minimize the benefits of a small amount of exercise or think that you aren't accomplishing anything. Research shows that doing 10 minutes of exercise three times a day brings similar benefits to doing 30 minutes at a time.

Taking a 10-minute walk or bike ride will usually give you an energy boost. At the same time, it will also sharpen your thinking, brighten your eyes, and lift your spirits.

It doesn't take a lot

With time, even a small amount of exercise will bring improvement. Think of it this way. If you walked just 10 minutes every day for one entire year, you would see major changes in your muscle tone, your weight, and your overall health.

While 10 minutes of activity certainly doesn't give the same benefits as 20 to 30 minutes, it may be the secret to getting you started back toward a consistent exercise plan.

TODAY

- Make a sign that says "10-Minute Solution."

- Post it where you'll see it right before you start to exercise (or decide not to exercise). Then choose an activity for today.

- Whether it's walking, riding a bike, swimming, or even playing croquet, do it for 10 minutes, then decide whether to stop or to continue. Either way, you're a success!

DAYS 41–50 COMPLETED!

You've come this far in your 100 days . . .

Don't stop now. If you're struggling to stick with it, push yourself to finish *one more day.* You'll immediately be another day closer to achieving your weight-loss goals.

Just do one more day!

❧ DAYS 51-60 ❧

EMOTIONAL EATING

DAY 51   What is emotional eating?

DAY 52   Food is an instant fix

DAY 53   Food is my best friend

DAY 54   Eating to feel better

DAY 55   Food is the consolation prize

DAY 56   Head hunger

DAY 57   Head hunger "insteads"

DAY 58   Heart hunger

DAY 59   Heart hunger "insteads"

DAY 60   Create a stop sign

☘ DAY 51 ☘

What is emotional eating?

You were doing so well, but then something went wrong. Maybe you became angry with your boss or upset with your kids. Perhaps you felt depressed about your finances or you struggled with a relationship problem. You knew you weren't hungry, but you reached for a few chips or cookies to make yourself feel better. You've just slipped into emotional eating.

Think about how many times you eat for reasons other than to fuel your body. Sneaking a candy bar in the middle of the afternoon, searching the cupboard when the kids go down for a nap, nibbling a free doughnut at the bank—all of these match the true definition.

Emotional eating:
Anytime you reach for food when you aren't
physically hungry or needing nutrition

There went the diet!

If you occasionally grab a candy bar on a stressful day, you probably won't do much damage. But if you aren't careful, you can slide into using food to "fix" your emotional needs. Eventually emotional eating will destroy your diet plan as well as ruin your motivation and your self-esteem.

To stop emotional eating, you first have to recognize you're doing it. Start paying attention to the times you eat when you truly aren't hungry. Analyze your habits such as having a bowl of ice cream every night at bedtime or grabbing a few cookies every time you get off the phone with your mother.

Why am I eating?

When you start thinking about food, decide whether you're having a physical need or an emotional one. Before you put anything in your mouth, ask yourself:

Is this hunger or a desire to eat?

If you decide you are hungry, give your body some fuel. But if you're having a *desire to eat,* catch yourself on the spot and ask: "What's going on here? What's making me want to eat right now?" Then consider how you could take care of your needs instead of appeasing them with food.

TODAY

- Make a sign that says, "Is this hunger or a desire to eat?"

- Whenever you want to eat something, pull out the sign. Then decide if you need fuel or if your food desire is related to your emotions.

- In your journal, make a list of situations or places where you are most likely to do emotional eating. Notice any patterns or specific times when you struggle with this.

☘ DAY 52 ☘

Food is an instant fix

Without a doubt, food provides a reliable instant fix. In our culture of fast-food restaurants and microwave ovens, you can almost always get your food cravings fulfilled instantly. And you never have to wait for relief. From the first bite of a cookie or candy bar, you can feel a nice sense of pleasure and satisfaction.

Food also provides a great source of entertainment. If there's nothing good on TV, you can always raid the refrigerator until the programming changes. In fact, it's easy to slip into *wandering around eating*—where you allow food to solve your problems of boredom or restlessness.

Food also becomes a solution to times when you have nothing to do. On a rainy afternoon or a long weekend with no plans, you might eat to fill up the empty time. As one of my clients admitted, "Without food, I'd have no fun at all!"

Procrastinate and escape

Eating provides a great way to procrastinate. When you face a task you don't want to do, food gives you a convenient escape. Suppose you need to study for a test, clean the house, or mow the lawn. You simply convince yourself that if you eat something first, you'll be able to tackle it more easily.

Sometimes you might use food to avoid beginning a task. If you have to complete a difficult project such as writing a report, heading for the refrigerator can help you pretend you don't have to do it. As a rule, the larger or more daunting the project, the more times you will eat to avoid it.

Eating to avoid life

Do you ever have times when you just don't feel like doing *anything?* Sometimes we reach for food because we're tired of all the demands in our lives. When you feel exhausted or emotionally worn down, eating is the only thing that doesn't seem to take any effort!

The next time this happens, identify exactly what you *don't feel like doing.* Then remind yourself: "The task will still be there after I finish my food, so I might as well go ahead and do it." Begin looking for healthier ways to manage your avoidance and then leave food out of the picture.

TODAY

- Identify times when you're most likely to eat in order to avoid doing something. Write these down in your journal. Then plan ways you could handle these tasks without eating something first.

- Notice any times today when you're tempted to use food as an instant fix.

- Record these thoughts and experiences as well.

※ DAY 53 ※
Food is my best friend

Most of the time, we don't really intend to do emotional eating. It's just that we're bored or lonely or stressed or angry or upset. We'd much rather have these emotions taken care of some other way—with arms around us, some appreciative words, even something interesting on TV. But when we search for solutions and come up empty, we're stuck with figuring out how to fix our own problems.

Food works for everything!
Eating does provide relief. Food entertains you when you're bored, gives you an outlet when you're mad, and heals your soul if you're sad or lonely. It helps you feel comforted and nurtured when life gets you down. It even provides a shield that protects you from uncomfortable emotions such as grief.

During times when you're feeling anxious or afraid, eating can provide stamina and boost your courage. For example, when you're at parties or social gatherings, you can hide your feelings behind a plate of snacks. If the uneasiness creeps back in, you can simply eat more. Food becomes the security blanket that gets you through the evening without having to deal with people or small-talk conversations.

Food can also boost your confidence when you're facing uncomfortable situations. Perhaps you always eat a snack before presenting a big project at work. Or you grab a few cookies when you have to call your ex-husband about the child-support payments. As long as you have food close by, you feel strong enough to deal with your issues.

Change the pattern

The truth is—*food works!* But when it's misused, it can also harm your weight and your health, making you resent the very solution it provides. Eventually food can become your *best friend,* the only way you know to fix your problems.

Take a look at your eating struggles. Do you feel out of control around food? Do you wish you had some other ways to manage your challenges? If you're hooked into using food to fix your emotional needs, it's time to change the pattern and learn new ways to handle these areas of your life.

TODAY

- Think about how you usually manage challenges or emotional needs. Do you often use food as your friend or as a way to cope with life?

- In your notebook, write down a list of times when food becomes your friend.

- Choose an item from your list and then plan how you could manage that issue without reaching for food. Record your ideas in your notebook.

❦ DAY 54 ❦
Eating to feel better

The words slip out so easily. "If I eat something, maybe I'll feel better." When you're tired, stressed, or physically ill, food is often the first thing that comes to mind. It tends to provide an appealing cure for everything from a cold or the flu to exhaustion after a long day of work.

Sometimes you really do need food. If you're tired because your body needs fuel, eating probably will make you feel better. But having an energy drop doesn't always mean it's time to eat. Make sure that you can recognize the difference between your fuel needs and wanting an emotional fix.

Why are you tired?

Before you stick your head into the refrigerator, analyze what else could be making you tired. If you need to calm down or de-stress, try doing a few deep-breathing exercises instead of eating. Give your eyes a rest from the computer or take a break from the task you're working on.

Recognize when you need rest, not food, and then go to bed, take a nap, or just close your eyes and give them a break for a few minutes. Sip a cup of hot tea or a diet soda and allow your body to relax. Remember that music can provide a powerful way to reenergize. You can match your music to your needs by listening to selections that have a quick, high-energy beat.

Instead of immediately reaching for food when you're feeling tired, do something else *first* and see if it takes care of the problem. Try these non-food methods for boosting your energy:

1. Move your body.

Instead of heading for your recliner after an exhausting day, go for a brief walk or do something else that gets you moving. Physical activity will usually revive you better than lying on the couch with chips and a soda. Also, drink more water or other fluids because being dehydrated can add to your fatigue.

2. Get some rest.

Put your feet up, take a nap (a lost art), or take time for a few minutes of meditation or stretching. Begin going to bed earlier. Force yourself to rest when you need it.

3. Distract yourself.

Do something that will take your mind off how you feel. Mentally escape with a book or a shopping trip. When you keep busy, you may find your tiredness lifts without a food fix. Make sure you choose a diversion that fills your mind, not empties it. Watching TV or playing computer games will often make you feel dull rather than revived.

TODAY

- Create an instant energy plan using specific types of fuel or activities that usually revive you.

- Watch for times when you need to take breaks in order to prevent pushing yourself to exhaustion.

- In your notebook, write a summary of your new energy plan.

❧ DAY 55 ❧

Food is the consolation prize

You probably didn't start out being an emotional eater. But as you were growing up, food began to show up almost everywhere. Soon it didn't seem to matter whether you were hungry or not—you ate anyway.

On your birthday, you blew out the candles, and everyone celebrated by eating chocolate cake. People encouraged you: "Eat some more; it's good for you," and they praised you for cleaning your plate. If you fell down, Mom gave you a cookie and your skinned knee magically stopped hurting.

It doesn't take a traumatic event or a bad childhood to get hooked into emotional eating. In fact, eating is one of the most common ways people cope with problems or struggles in life. You simply learned that whenever you have a tough time, food always makes you feel better.

The link between food and emotions

If you always reach for something to eat when you don't like how you feel, you eventually create a link between food and your emotional needs. And it seems to work. But at some point, overeating numbs your feelings, and you can stop noticing what's missing in your life. Food simply provides a legal, socially acceptable way to escape from reality.

Although eating may temporarily soothe an emotional need, unfortunately the end result never matches your dream. Food becomes the *consolation prize*. It's better than nothing, but not even close to what you really wanted—to be loved, appreciated, or comforted.

What you actually want

There are many days that you'd give anything for someone to hold you or to offer kind, encouraging words. You want somebody to care that you have a bad cold or that your car broke down for the third time this month. You wish life were different—that you had more money, more love, or more fun. When you don't get these things, it's easy to look for something (such as food) to take their place.

When you reach for something to eat but know you aren't hungry, stop and ask yourself: "What do I *really* want or need?" Remind yourself that food will only be the consolation prize. Then think about how you can address your needs in some other way instead of expecting food to take care of them.

TODAY

- Recall any recent times when you ate in order to feel better. Perhaps at a family gathering, you used food to fill your need for love and acceptance. Or maybe you reached for a snack to calm your anger or frustration at work.

- In your journal or notebook, describe any of your experiences with emotional eating.

- Even if you initially felt better, consider whether the food really met your needs or if it was just the *consolation prize*. Then identify what you really wanted.

⚖ DAY 56 ⚖

Head hunger

Have you ever wondered why some days you would kill for a piece of cheesecake, yet at other times you seem to crave tortilla chips or peanuts? You may not realize it, but with non-hungry eating, your food choices can serve as a mirror, indicating what type of emotional need you're experiencing.

In my work I've learned you can separate emotional eating into two distinct types—*head hunger* and *heart hunger*. We'll look at head hunger today, then address heart hunger later.

Chewy, crunchy foods

Head hunger usually starts with a *specific* food thought or craving; you know *exactly* what you want. A food desire pops into your mind, making you search for chips, popcorn, or a specific brand of candy bar.

With head hunger, you typically look for foods that are *chewy* or *crunchy*, such as potato chips, nuts, and candy. Foods with a dense, chewy texture also seem to appease head hunger. For example, hamburgers, pizza, and even chocolate all have a "smash in your mouth" sensation that replaces what you'd really like to do to somebody or something else.

Head hunger usually tends to be connected to pressure-type emotions such as anger, frustration, or resentment. It can also show up when you're trying to *avoid* feelings that you don't like such as grief or other painful emotions. Some of the most common reasons for head hunger eating include stress, deadlines, and other people.

What do I want to chew on?

Whenever you crave a chewy or crunchy food, take a quick inventory of what might be affecting you. Then ask yourself, *"What do I really want to chew on?"*

Try to identify anything that's irritating you, bothering you, or stressing you out right at that moment. Your answer might include your kids, finances, friends, project deadlines, or a new or difficult job.

When you've identified the source of your head hunger, ask yourself: "Will eating change this issue?" In other words, will food really mend your relationships or improve your child's behavior? Can it eliminate a project deadline? Of course not.

Eating might seem to fix the problem because initially you feel calmer or less angry. But after you finish eating and the food is gone, the situation still remains—often causing you to reach for food again. Eating simply postpones what you really need to do in order to cope with life issues.

TODAY

- Make a list of your favorite *chewy* or *crunchy* foods, especially ones that you might reach for when you aren't physically hungry.

- Think of at least three places or situations where you're tempted to reach for head hunger foods.

- Ask yourself what you really want to "chew on" in those situations. Record your insights in your notebook.

❧ DAY 57 ❧
Head hunger "insteads"

You don't need a complicated diet plan in order to manage head hunger cravings. You just need quick solutions that will keep you from heading to the cupboard.

Today you'll start creating a resource list of things and ideas you can draw on *instead* of eating. Your "instead" activities won't solve the problem of emotional eating, but they'll place buffers between you and the issues that tempt you to eat.

What's causing my hunger?

When you realize you're facing a head hunger craving, stop to think about the real cause of your hunger and how you might address your emotional needs. Then do one of the items from your list *before* you eat anything.

Keep the list readily available so you can draw from it any-time. When you get caught off guard by unexpected emotional issues, use your "insteads" to interrupt the automatic response of using food to take care of your feelings.

Pick your "insteads"

Here are some ideas to get you started with your "insteads." Choose the ones that fit for you and then add more of your own.

- Jump up and down to shake loose your anger or your frustration.

- Read something. Plan ahead so that you'll have a couple of good "diversion" books ready to grab.

- Take several deep breaths. Sigh loudly with each one.

- *Wait 10 minutes* before eating anything. During that time, do something positive such as read to your child or offer encouragement to a troubled friend.

- Read a few pages in a joke book. Laugh until you aren't feeling upset anymore.

- Do something that takes a lot of concentration, such as a crossword puzzle.

- Sing loudly, even if you don't consider yourself a singer.

- Yell at your steering wheel.

- Play the piano or a musical instrument.

- Call a friend and ask for five minutes of talk time.

- Type a letter to someone you want to chew on. Explain in great detail why you are upset. Then burn the letter or delete it from your computer files.

- Journal your feelings. Write the words, "I want to chew on the following . . ." and then list as many things as you can think of.

TODAY

- In your notebook, create an "instead" list for head hunger. Include any activities or diversions that would help you postpone eating for a while.

- Post copies of your list in places where you can draw from it quickly, such as in your daily calendar or on your bathroom mirror.

- Use at least two of your "insteads" today.

❧ DAY 58 ❧
Heart hunger

Do you ever have times when you want something to eat but have no idea what you want? With *heart hunger,* the second type of emotional eating, you don't usually get a specific food craving—you just start thinking about eating.

As you begin searching your cupboard or the refrigerator, you're unsure of what sounds good at the moment. You just know you want something. Anytime you want to eat but don't know what you want, think *heart hunger.*

When you finally decide what you want, heart hunger will usually send you toward soft, smooth, or creamy foods such as ice cream, doughnuts, or pasta. It can also make you want comfort foods or ones related to fond memories or happy times.

Empty emotions

Heart hunger usually stems from *empty* emotions, such as feeling depressed, discouraged, or lonely. It can also show up when you're bored or restless, as well as times when you feel hurt, disappointed, or let down. Sometimes heart hunger will relate to yearning for things such as attention or appreciation.

When you realize that you're experiencing heart hunger, ask yourself: *"What's making me feel empty right now? What am I missing or needing in my life?"* Are you feeling alone and wishing you had more friends or a new life partner? Maybe difficult situations have left you tired and discouraged or feeling depressed. Perhaps you don't have much challenge or meaning in your life, making you bored or restless.

Comfort foods

Sometimes heart hunger sneaks into your daily life without your realizing it. For example, do you eat a bowl of ice cream most nights before you go to bed? For many people, ice cream relates back to childhood memories or to nostalgia for family connections. Other types of heart hunger foods such as cinnamon rolls or brownies can fill the empty spots left by broken relationships or disappointments in life.

Before you reach for the first bite of comfort food, think about what feels empty or missing in your life. Then ask yourself, "Will eating change this?"

Of course, sometimes eating *does* make things feel better, at least for a while. But in the end, nothing changes. Your real life is still there, filled with the same emptiness as before.

TODAY

- Which foods are you most likely to eat when you're having heart hunger?

- Write these down in your notebook, and then make a list of the situations that might send you toward heart hunger eating.

- Watch for times when you want something to eat but don't know what you want. During these times, try to identify what's missing or empty and then do something to respond to what you really need.

❧ DAY 59 ❧
Heart hunger "insteads"

You've already created a list of ideas for managing head hunger. Now you need to come up with a similar group of activities that will help you appease heart hunger. As you build this list of "insteads," look for things you can draw from immediately when you feel tempted to eat.

Filling empty emotions

When you're facing the pressure emotions of *head* hunger, active things such as exercise or yelling at the steering wheel will usually work best. But with *heart* hunger, you may want solutions that feel more nurturing or soothing, such as a warm bath or a massage.

Look for ways to match heart hunger activities with the type of need you're having. During times you feel sad or lonely, you might find solace in listening to music or reading a good book. If you tend to get bored easily, consider learning a new hobby or taking a class to awaken your brain.

Heart hunger "insteads"

As you build your list of heart hunger "insteads," don't worry if some of the things are similar to the ones you chose for managing head hunger. Simply create a list that fits for you, and then start using it immediately. Here are some ideas:

- Hold or stroke a live animal. Cats and dogs often make wonderful therapists.

- Take a warm bath or a hot shower.
- Hug or hold somebody. If necessary, hug a teddy bear or other stuffed animal.
- Do gardening or other activities that involve nature.
- Get a massage. If that's not an option for you, massage your own hands or feet.
- Read inspirational books or happy stories that will help brighten your spirits.
- Light lots of candles, especially ones with your favorite fragrances.
- Cry. Let yourself go until you feel as if you're finished.
- Give yourself a flower reward. Buy many inexpensive ones and surround yourself with them.
- Buy yourself a greeting card and pretend it came from your best friend. Write a love note in it and sign it.
- Write your own job evaluation. Say all the wonderful things you need to hear from your boss. Praise every aspect of your work in great detail.
- Listen to a favorite tape or CD. Indulgently do nothing while you listen.

TODAY

- In your notebook, create an "instead" list for heart hunger. Think of any activities or diversions that would provide comfort or nurturing.
- Make several copies of your list, and then put them in places where you can draw from them quickly.
- Use at least two of them today.

❧ DAY 60 ❧
Create a stop sign

By regularly drawing from your "instead" lists for head hunger and heart hunger, you'll be able to avoid many of your emotional eating struggles right from the start. But to use all of these tools effectively, you also need an instant reaction plan, sort of an "emotional stop sign," to remind yourself of your good intentions.

Instant response plan

Most emergency or firehouse crews rely on a process they've planned out in advance. When a call comes in, staff members immediately stop whatever they're doing and begin using the countdown for tackling the challenge in front of them.

You can develop a similar "stop everything" response to help you manage your food struggles. From your head hunger and heart hunger lists of things to do instead of eating, select a few that are your favorites. Examples might include grabbing a piece of gum, taking a short walk, or writing in your journal for five minutes.

Use these as your *stop signs,* sort of an emergency countdown plan for emotional hunger. You might want to create one list for head hunger and a different one for heart hunger. Plan that each of your stop signs will include three items.

Anytime you're tempted to reach for food, pull out one of your stop signs and do the three things on your list. Carry your lists with you or, better yet, memorize them so you can draw on them instantly whenever the need arises.

Emergency stop signs

Think of situations where you start eating before you even think about what you're doing. Then plan an emergency stop sign that you can use every time you're in that setting. For example, here's how you might use a stop sign to avoid eating M&M's every day right after getting home from work.

The minute I start reaching for the bag of M&M's:

- Walk, walk, walk. Do something active.

- Take at least three deep breaths. With each one keep telling myself, "I am strong!"

- Put a stick of gum in my mouth to stop my food thoughts.

Once you decide to use your stop sign, do it quickly— before you change your mind. Don't let your resolve weaken or try to convince yourself a little bit of food won't hurt you. In many cases, the food does hurt you by increasing your emotional struggles or by harming your self-esteem.

TODAY

- In your journal, write down three things you will use as your "stop sign" plan for handling emotional hunger. Create separate lists for head hunger and heart hunger.

- Copy your stop signs onto a billfold-sized card, and then carry them with you as an instant reminder.

- Share your lists with a buddy and agree that you'll both use them as a set of emergency coping skills.

DAYS 51–60 COMPLETED!

You've come this far in your 100 days . . .

Don't stop now. If you're struggling to stick with it, push yourself to finish *one more day.* You'll immediately be another day closer to achieving your weight-loss goals.

Just do one more day!

❧ DAYS 61–70 ❧

TRIGGERS AND WORD PLAY

DAY 61   Food triggers

DAY 62   Non-food triggers

DAY 63   Buffers

DAY 64   Instant tools for triggers

DAY 65   Stimulus narrowing

DAY 66   Don't even start!

DAY 67   Never say "I blew it"

DAY 68   I had a "pause"

DAY 69   No cheating allowed

DAY 70   No good or bad

☘ DAY 61 ☘
Food triggers

Food cues or *triggers* include all those little signals and thoughts that prompt you to eat during times when you weren't planning on it. When you open the refrigerator door to get a can of soda, you glimpse a tasty leftover. Even though you weren't the slightest bit hungry, seeing the food makes you want to eat it.

Types of triggers

Both the sight and smell of food can be powerful triggers that make you want to eat. Think about the aroma of steaks on the grill, your mom's pot roast, or fresh cinnamon rolls. And have you ever noticed how theaters always seem to have the popcorn machine in action right before a movie starts?

Discussing recipes or watching cooking shows may set off a desire that lingers until you get out your baking pans. Even talking about how to *avoid* food can prompt the desire to eat. Many weight-loss group members have sheepishly confessed that they go out to eat immediately after their meetings end.

All of these food cues can suddenly make you remember you were "hungry." Then once you start eating, the taste of food becomes another trigger, causing you to eat more.

Food sights, smells, and tastes are easy triggers to recognize. But visual images such as billboards or TV ads that *remind* you of food can also crumble your resolve. One minute you weren't thinking about food or eating at all. The next minute you can't *stop* thinking about it.

Subtle food triggers

Any activities that you've connected with food in the past can easily trigger you to repeat these patterns. Going to parties and happy hour gatherings, or being at family reunions, can all prompt eating struggles. Maybe your friends often go out for pizza or meet for dinner at a particular restaurant. You eat with them because "it's what we always do."

Instead of slapping your head right after you give in to a food trigger, learn how to recognize these cues *before* you eat. During the next few days, you'll learn a variety of techniques for handling triggers without automatically responding to them.

TODAY

- Watch for any food cues that show up during your day. Notice the triggers from billboards, break rooms, people's desks, magazine covers, food discussions, and even your own thoughts, such as what to fix for dinner.

- For today, focus specifically on triggers that relate to food, such as sights and smells or other things that remind you of food.

- In your journal, make note of any specific food triggers or situations that tempted you today.

⚜ DAY 62 ⚜
Non-food triggers

You probably don't have much trouble identifying eating triggers related to food itself. But as you know, many non-food triggers can also pull you toward eating. People, situations, or even habits you've previously associated with food can easily send you to the refrigerator or the cupboard.

Uncomfortable emotions, demands from others, or even high expectations of yourself can all trigger unplanned eating. So can the need for relief from pain, illness, fatigue, or other physical discomfort.

Habits that involve food

Some food patterns can turn into habits, always tempting you to eat when you're in certain settings. Think about some of your routines, such as having ice cream at bedtime, snacking as soon as you arrive home from work, or eating in the car.

Perhaps every time you go to a movie, you think about eating popcorn. Or whenever you have to face a difficult employee, you automatically head for some food.

It's also common to experience many different triggers at the same time. Perhaps you were feeling depressed or upset and then you went to a meeting in a conference room filled with snacks, such as doughnuts, cookies, and chips.

In this setting, you're tempted by the sight and the smell of food as well as your desire to connect with team members. Without giving it a thought, you join right in with the rest of the staff as they munch away on the cookies and chips.

Emotions as triggers

Emotional needs you've associated with food in the past can also trigger your eating desires. Maybe you routinely head for the refrigerator after getting your job review or a nasty telephone call from your ex-spouse.

Emotional triggers can often be very subtle and hidden. You might not realize you're feeling depressed or bored until you start searching for food. The same thing is true with stress, anger, loneliness, or depression. These emotional needs can send you toward food simply because eating helped fix them in the past.

Because non-food triggers aren't always very obvious, watch carefully for the signals that cause you to want food. As you go through your day, pay attention to the subtle cues that prompt your food thoughts or send you hunting for a snack.

TODAY

- Notice all of the non-food cues that tempt you to eat. In particular, watch for how you respond to stress, anger, and other intense emotions.

- Write down a list of any food thoughts that were prompted by emotions or other non-food triggers.

- Notice whether you typically give in to emotional triggers or whether you're able to ignore them.

✵ DAY 63 ✵
Buffers

In your efforts to manage your food triggers, one of the best techniques is to create *buffers* that will protect you from slipping into eating. Whenever possible, put some distance between you and your high-risk, problem foods. Instead of trying so hard to improve your willpower, simply don't allow yourself to be tempted in the first place.

Look closely at the purpose of certain food items such as the candy jar on your desk. Is it there because you have a strong need to be liked or accepted? If so, look for some new ways to connect with others such as handing out free flowers once a week or sharing books you enjoy.

Don't tempt yourself

As many people do, Laura had a hard time resisting peanut butter, and when she had it in her cupboard, she'd eat lots of it. She said, "Whenever I would bring peanut butter into my house, I'd keep dipping into it, and in three days I'd finish off the whole jar. Now I don't buy it anymore so it's not around to tempt me."

Just as in Laura's decision, sometimes the easiest buffer is to protect yourself from the food in the first place. If you tend to give in to foods such as chips, cookies, or candy, don't stock them in your home or your work setting.

I've personally struggled with crunchy snack foods, such as potato chips. Finally my husband and I agreed that we'd stop bringing them into our home. As a result, I haven't bought potato chips or had them in my house for more than a decade.

Stop triggers before they start

If you're determined to change your life, make a clean sweep of trigger foods around you. Most people who quit smoking don't keep packs of cigarettes around to see whether they can resist them. Treat food the same way—get rid of what puts you at risk for giving in and overeating.

And don't try using your children as an excuse by saying, "It isn't fair they can't have snack foods in the house." Instead, teach kids to share in your goal of healthy eating. For times when they want tempting snacks, have them eat those foods in places that are out of your sight.

TODAY

- Eliminate one trigger from your life. Choose one food or category of food and make the decision to protect yourself from it. This doesn't mean you never eat it, but that you avoid having it around most of the time.

- Clear that item from all of your regular storage places, including your home, car, office, and even your shopping list.

- In your notebook, list the food trigger that you've eliminated as well as others you need to protect yourself from in the future.

❧ DAY 64 ❧

Instant tools for triggers

Suppose you have a really bad day. Next thing you know, you start eating and feel as though you can't stop. In this case, you need a fast solution—an instant tool—for getting away from whatever triggered you to eat.

First, stop thinking you can't resist food temptations. Just because you see a delicious-looking piece of cheesecake does *not* mean you have to eat it. In the same way, you don't have to let the smell of popcorn ruin your afternoon. Instead, learn how to be prepared for these situations by having instant tools readily available.

Brush your teeth

Once you start eating certain foods such as nuts or candy, their taste or texture can become almost addicting. When a taste trigger hooks you into continuous eating, you can usually stop it instantly by the simple act of brushing your teeth.

Regardless of what foods you've been eating, brushing your teeth completely changes the flavors in your mouth. After you eliminate those food sensations, you can usually prevent the taste trigger from tempting you again.

If you aren't in a situation where you can brush your teeth, try eating something with the distinct opposite flavor of what you're hooked on. For example, to block a sweet or salty taste, consider sucking on a lemon wedge or eating a dill pickle. To eliminate spicy or garlicky food triggers such as salsa, reach for a stick of gum or a strong mint-flavored candy.

Flee when necessary

Create a "fire escape plan" that will work anytime you feel overly tempted by food. Learn ways to say *no* when friends, family, or coworkers push you to eat. Also remember the "not just yet" line you learned on Day 6. Whenever you need an immediate escape, pull out this phrase and use it to sneak away without having to explain.

Recognize times when you feel weak and you're about to lose the battle against a food trigger. When this happens, get away from all food—take a walk, go home, leave the room, even go to bed if necessary.

TODAY

- In your notebook, write a list of situations, foods, or emotions that often trigger you to eat.

- Identify triggers that are hardest for you to resist. Perhaps you get hooked by movie popcorn or TV ads. Maybe it's your mother's baking or goodies in the break room at work.

- Make a "fire escape plan" for each of your most common triggers. Record this in your notebook.

❈ DAY 65 ❈

Stimulus narrowing

Each time you encounter a food cue or temptation, you eventually decide whether to *eat* or *not eat*. But in most cases, you have only a split second to make this decision. The faster you say "No!" and turn away from the food, the more likely you'll be able to avoid giving in.

Suppose you notice a large chocolate brownie in the break room at work. If you stare at it, yearn for it, or keep thinking about it, you weaken your ability to resist eating it. On the other hand, if you make a firm decision to skip eating the brownie, then focus on your resolve and you'll discover the food loses its power.

Don't think too long

This concept, called "stimulus narrowing," works because it completely eliminates the possibility of changing your mind. Think about some of the food cues you typically encounter during your day. As you face each one of them, *immediately* decide that you will *not eat,* and then stick with your decision.

Jean noticed her finicky son had left all of his scalloped corn on his plate. It looked awfully good, so after her family left the kitchen, she began clearing the table, still eyeing the corn. She left her son's plate until last, then finally picked it up and carried it toward the sink.

As she began to scrape his food into the garbage disposal, Jean stared longingly at the corn one more time. It looked so good . . . Suddenly she grabbed a fork and before she could stop herself, she shoveled the corn into her mouth.

Later Jean said, "I knew I wanted to eat that corn from the moment I saw it was left on his plate. I should have dumped it immediately instead of contemplating whether to eat it."

Say no and mean it

Don't let thoughts about eating weaken your resolve. When you're tempted by a certain food, tell yourself: *"No, I won't eat it!"* Then immediately get away from the situation and don't allow your thoughts to go back to it. You'll find that as you gain strength against your unplanned eating, you'll also decrease the mental anguish of fighting to maintain control.

TODAY

- Watch for food cues that have the potential to hook you into overeating. Like a parent speaking to a child, firmly tell yourself "no" on the spot.

- Then walk away, get busy with something else, and affirm that you won't go back to the food. In your notebook, record how this experience felt.

- Stay strong in your resolve. Don't keep whining until you wear down your resistance and give in.

☘ DAY 66 ☘
Don't even start!

Setting limits for yourself regarding certain food items can give you power over temptation. But at times you may need to go even one step further in order to protect yourself from getting hooked by the taste of a food.

With sweets, desserts, and snack foods, the first bite is often what sets you up for wanting more. So if you can prevent yourself from taking that very first bite, you'll be able to escape the instant taste trigger that weakens your resolve.

But how do you do this when a tempting food is calling your name? First, work on creating a strong self-talk plan. Make a decision that you won't eat even *one bite* of the enticing food item. Then come up with a variety of phrases that you can say to yourself again and again to strengthen your resistance.

Self-talk messages

Suppose you're at a party with bowls of nuts and M&M's on tables all around the room. Whenever you're about to reach into one of the bowls, immediately stop yourself with a firm, stimulus-narrowing message that says, *"Don't even start!"* Repeat this phrase again and again until you feel totally in control around the food.

You can decide what type of mental voice works best. Maybe you prefer soft words that feel kind and gentle. Or you might use a strong, parental tone that's fierce and insistent. Just make sure your words keep you from even tasting the food. By avoiding that very first bite, you'll be able to prevent the taste trigger from getting started.

Invent more lines

You can come up with a variety of self-talk phrases that work to protect you around food temptations. In addition to the powerful phrase "Don't even start," consider using:

- Don't even go there!

- Stay on top of your plan.

- Hold your goals up high.

- Live above the crowd.

Play with your self-talk phrases until you find the ones that are most effective for you. Every time you are determined to avoid a food entirely, use your own firm self-talk as a way to instantly stop yourself from eating.

TODAY

- Look for a situation in which you might be tempted to eat a snack or dessert, then intentionally *don't eat any.*

- Repeat a strong phrase such as "Don't even start" several times inside your head. Keep using this message to protect yourself from the first bite.

- Walk away from the food and then congratulate yourself on a new level of success with managing temptation.

☘ DAY 67 ☘

Never say "I blew it"

One of the most common dieting phrases is, *"I've already blown it, so I might as well go ahead and eat the rest."* But each time you say "I blew it," you reinforce your sense of failure and disappointment with not staying on your plan. You also give yourself permission to follow a minor slipup with a major eating binge.

Sometimes people take this further by planning even more damage. I recently watched a woman at an ice cream shop as she ordered a large hot-fudge sundae. When asked if she wanted whipped cream and nuts, she responded, "Sure! I'm blowing it anyway, so I might as well go for all of it."

Pay for it by more eating

When you think you've "blown it," you may decide you should punish yourself by eating even more. Although you feel bloated and miserable, you make yourself pay by pushing in more food, which makes you feel even worse.

Here's how Beverly described her punishing routine with food. "It's as if I backed my car into a post. But instead of assessing the damage and driving away, I decide one dent isn't enough. So to punish myself for my first mistake, I slam my car backward into the post again and again."

Phrases such as "I blew it" emphasize discouragement and failure. Throw these old dieting lines out the window and begin using a kinder, more gentle voice when you talk to yourself.

Starting now, resolve that you'll never say "I blew it" again in regard to your eating or your weight-loss efforts.

A minor event

Don't let yourself get caught up in your old ways of thinking. One mistake doesn't have to ruin your entire plan. Instead of treating a slipup as a crisis, learn to view it as a minor event. Come up with a neutral way to describe your eating struggle. For example, you might say to yourself: "Isn't that interesting? I wonder what that was all about."

Then look at your eating struggle and see if you can figure out what contributed to it. Were there any emotional issues that might have prompted you to head to the refrigerator or grab the cookies? After you see what's behind your eating pattern, you can focus on taking care of those needs instead of reaching for food.

TODAY

- Resolve that you will never again describe your eating by saying the words "I blew it."

- Invent some new phrases that acknowledge your eating struggle but at the same time encourage you to move forward. Consider using statements such as, "That was minor, so I need to keep it that way."

- Record your favorite phrases in your notebook and memorize them so you can use them immediately whenever you have a slipup.

☙ DAY 68 ☙

I had a "pause"

As you work on changing your dieting vocabulary, here's another way to eliminate saying "I blew it." Anytime you slip up and eat something that's not on your diet plan, skip beating yourself up with harsh, punishing words.

Instead, label the incident as a *pause* in your diet plan. This kind, nonjudgmental word doesn't make any detrimental references to your personality or your ability to accomplish a goal. Instead, it allows you to take a break in your efforts, then rest and regroup.

Having a pause

Imagine that you're taking a hike in the mountains, slowly winding up a trail that eventually leads you to a scenic view. About an hour into the hike, you begin feeling a little tired and a bit thirsty.

At this point, you stop walking and sit down on a large rock to take a couple of sips from your water bottle. After resting a few minutes and catching your breath, you stand up and return to the trail.

You would not say, "Look how awful I am! I told you I couldn't do a hike. I guess I'll just lie down on this rock and give up." You also wouldn't punish yourself by saying, "Since I blew the hike, I have to go back a few hundred yards and walk that part over again!"

Instead, you would view this brief rest as a *pause* in your hiking efforts. After your break, you would get back up and continue your journey.

Erase the board

Use this same approach with your weight-loss program. If you slip up on your diet plan, simply say, "I had a brief pause, but now I'm back on track."

Then after you've acknowledged your pause, don't get stuck dwelling on it. Instead, look carefully at your slipup, learn from it, and then let it go. To increase your ability to do this, practice erasing the incident from your head.

Suppose you gobbled ten cookies instead of the two you had originally planned to eat. Picture a white erasable board and mentally write on it, "I ate ten cookies."

Spend a few minutes thinking about what got in the way of your original eating plan. Then when you've learned from that event, mentally erase the board and get on with your life.

TODAY

- Next time you're tempted to say "I blew it," stop yourself immediately. Instead, label your slipup as a *pause*.

- Decide how you will bounce back from an eating pause. Write down a short plan that includes what you'll say to yourself as well as what you'll do next.

- Whenever you slip up, instead of dwelling on it, practice the skill of "erasing the board." Think about how you can learn from a pause rather than finding ways to punish yourself.

❧ DAY 69 ❧

No cheating allowed

I cheated big-time on my diet today. Does this phrase sound familiar? You've probably used several variations of this line. In fact, chances are that at some point you've said the word *cheat* when discussing your weight-loss efforts.

If you confess that you "cheated" on your diet, that indicates you believe the diet is in charge. You also label yourself in a way that gives away your power. After all, if you were strong, you wouldn't cheat on your program.

No more cheating

The truth is, you can't cheat with food! It's impossible. The word *cheat* refers to something illegal or immoral, and food is neither of these. You do not have some kind of moral or character defect just because you ate a cookie.

As of today, completely stop using the word *cheat* when you refer to your eating plan. Instead, use the words *choose* or *choice* to describe your behavior.

Each day you make dozens of choices in life, and how you eat is just one of them. You choose things such as what time to get up, whether to go to work, and how to talk to the people around you. You might not like all of your options, but the choices you make determine the outcomes of your day.

In regard to eating, every morsel that goes into your mouth is put there by choice. Sometimes you'll make healthy choices, sometimes lousy ones. With time, all of these choices affect your outcomes, such as whether or not you lose weight.

Making healthy choices

Instead of saying you cheated on your diet, admit to yourself that every time you reach for food, you're making choices. If you eat a cookie that wasn't on your plan, then say, "I *chose* to eat a cookie today." Maybe you wish you hadn't done it, but either way, you made a choice about eating it.

In addition, don't try to excuse your behavior by blaming lack of willpower or discipline. You're in charge of your own choices. Take responsibility for the decisions you make around food, and then when you talk about your actions, describe them in ways that maintain your personal power.

TODAY

- Talk to someone about your diet plan, using the word *choice* several times to describe your actions. Notice how that feels.

- In your journal, record at least three choices you made around food today.

- If you make a weak or poor choice, figure out how to describe it without using negative words such as *cheat*.

☘ DAY 70 ☘
No good or bad

I started the day being so good, but then someone brought a birth-day cake to the office and I was really bad. Have you ever described your eating behavior this way? Maybe you've even told someone about your vacation or a holiday weekend by confessing, "I was so bad the whole time."

Since eating is not a moral issue, you can't apply behavioral codes to what you do with food. Eating cookies or potato chips doesn't make you a bad person. The truth is that with eating, it's impossible to be *good* or *bad*. So from now on, stop using those words to describe yourself based on your food intake.

Who said it was bad?

One of the challenges with dieting is the way we categorize food in the first place. For example, who decided that a carrot was good and a brownie was bad? In most cases you simply measure your dieting efforts against a list of foods that are *allowed* or *not allowed*, then chastise yourself for eating from the wrong side.

To break the habit of calling yourself *good* or *bad*, follow the same logic as you did with cheating. When you discuss your weight-loss plan, refer to your eating choices.

With this new approach, you say, "I made a good choice this morning by eating a healthy breakfast. This afternoon, I made a poorer choice when I ate three brownies." By talking about each of your actions as a *choice*, you can eliminate the punishing self-messages that say you were bad.

100 DAYS OF WEIGHT LOSS

Change your vocabulary

Getting rid of old dieting terms such as *cheat, good,* and *bad* will take practice. At first you may feel awkward saying "I made some poor choices today."

But by changing your language, you take back your power around food. You also acknowledge that you are personally responsible for your decisions about what you eat.

TODAY

- In your journal, write a sentence or two about the choices you made today.

- Notice how often you hear other people use words such as *cheating, good,* and *bad* when discussing diet efforts. Each time you hear someone use these terms, mentally rewrite the sentences in a way that refers to choices in life.

- Teach this concept to a friend or diet buddy. Catch the times when either of you slips up by saying *cheat, good,* or *bad* to describe your eating patterns or food intake. Have a contest and designate the person who says these phrases the fewest times as the winner.

DAYS 61–70 COMPLETED!

You've come this far in your 100 days . . .

Don't stop now. If you're struggling to stick with it, push yourself to finish *one more day.* You'll immediately be another day closer to achieving your weight-loss goals.

Just do one more day!

❧ DAYS 71–80 ❧

GROWING STRONGER

✣ DAY 71 ✣

It's too hard!

Every few months Joanne would decide she was ready to lose weight. She'd gear up by saying, "This time, I will stay on my diet perfectly, I'll walk every day, and I'll never eat when I'm not hungry."

On her chosen day (always on a Monday), Joanne would begin her diet plan. Initially, she would do great—measuring and weighing her food, writing in her journal, and declining lunch invitations. But when unexpected events or other difficulties came up, she'd struggle to stay on her plan.

It seemed that demands from her work, her family, even her dog made every day a challenge. Finally Joanne would give up on her diet, saying, "I just can't do it. It's too hard!"

And she's right. For most people, it's extremely difficult to stick with goals of healthier eating and exercising. No one is ever immune from bad days, stress, and fatigue. And the ongoing challenges of life events can certainly make it hard to stay on your plan.

But that's not a good reason for giving up! Instead, you need to learn how to face the tough times without allowing them to pull you off track.

"I can do hard things!"

If you're like most people, you've done many hard things in your life. Giving birth, working at a job, moving to a new city, even cleaning the house—all of these fit the description. In reality, *you can do hard things!*

156

So instead of caving in on your diet because it feels too hard, buck up and tell yourself: "Of course it's hard. But I've done a lot of difficult things in my life, and this isn't any different. I know that *I can do hard things!*"

Be willing to do the work

There's no way to avoid it—losing weight takes a lot of effort. You have to plan meals, track what you eat, and avoid food temptations. Sometimes you have to make difficult decisions, tackle challenges, and manage people or situations that feel extremely difficult. But if you can find the courage and the focus to put up with the hard parts, you'll reach the goals you want so badly.

TODAY

- In your notebook, write, "I can do hard things."

- Make a list of hard things you've done in the past. Remind yourself that you are a strong person.

- Renew your commitment to doing the work that's involved in this project. Tell yourself you can do hard things, including staying on your diet and your exercise plan. Then do it.

☘ DAY 72 ☘
Sneak eating

Do you eat perfectly around others but creep off alone to finish off the last of the cookies or the leftover dessert? Maybe you keep a secret stash of your favorite candy so you can nibble it when no one is around. Even though you know that sneak eating can totally ruin your diet, you may still be struggling with it on a daily basis.

Maybe you've tried telling yourself that sneaking food doesn't matter that much. But behind this secret lies a huge range of emotions such as anger, resentment, and fear.

Perhaps you feel embarrassed or ashamed to be seen eating certain foods because of your weight. And if you've told people that you're on a diet, you probably don't want them to see you slipping up on your plan.

Sometimes you might just want to escape the prying eyes of the "diet police." Perhaps you're really tired of hearing your mother's negative comments about your weight. Or you're afraid your spouse will criticize you for eating certain foods.

Who are you really punishing?

If you feel pressured to follow your diet perfectly, you may attempt to punish other people by eating when they can't see you. And if you're subjected to constant monitoring or criticism from family members, you might secretly think, "I'll show you! There's no way you can control me now." Of course, you always end up punishing the wrong person. When you sneak food and overeat, you're the one who gains weight or feels bloated and miserable.

Eat in the presence of others

To overcome your patterns of sneak eating, consider making a policy that you'll always eat sweets or favorite foods in the presence of at least *one other person*. This means you can't dig into an entire carton of ice cream or finish off the rest of the Valentine's Day chocolates without someone watching you.

While you can get around this rule by going out to eat at a restaurant, it might not seem worth the effort. And if you know you're allowed to eat cookie dough only when you're around your mother, you'll probably just skip it.

To reinforce your decision, let others know you plan to never eat certain foods in private, then ask for their support. Also, remind them you'll be using tools such as the first two bites and savoring. And when you eat in their presence, ask them to offer you encouragement rather than criticism.

TODAY

- Make a list of foods as well as the situations that might prompt you to sneak eat.

- What are you saying to others when you sneak food? Are you secretly expressing anger or a need for control? In your notebook, write down some of the emotional needs you might be solving by sneak eating.

- Add a few thoughts about the ways people act when you don't follow your diet perfectly. Notice whether you react with fear, anger, resentment, or some other emotions.

❧ DAY 73 ❧
All-or-nothing

Do you ever struggle with being a perfectionist in your dieting efforts? Most people who are perfectionists tend to be all-or-nothing thinkers who follow the principle, *do it right or don't do it at all*. But since they never reach the point where they're able to do it *right,* true perfectionists never start.

When you get hung up on the *right* way to do things, you can lose sight of all the other possibilities. And if you're a true perfectionist, you not only apply the "do it right" concept to yourself, you also expect others to follow the same rules.

Embrace the gray

Perfectionism typically involves black-and-white thinking. Either you do the whole thing (white), or you don't do it at all (black). Between these two extremes lies a small gray area, a place that perfectionists hate to enter.

To decrease your struggles with perfectionism, you don't need to move entirely from one extreme to the other. You just need to be willing to put one foot into the gray.

By letting go of some of your perfectionist rules and rigid expectations, you'll be able to achieve a much healthier balance in nearly every area of your life. You will also find that you can manage your diet and exercise plan much easier.

So instead of expecting yourself to never eat sugar or to eat only when you're hungry, allow for a few exceptions. Look for ways you can settle for a small amount of progress yet still manage to feel successful.

Perfectionism is a gift!

Being a perfectionist isn't all bad. Often, it can help you accomplish things you wouldn't achieve otherwise. If you want to become healthier around your perfectionism, start treating it as a wonderful gift. Now you have to decide when to use your gift and when to store it on a shelf. With this approach, you can draw on your perfectionism when it matters, but at other times, choose to let it go.

You might also set a goal of striving for *excellence* instead of perfection. Because it's possible to achieve excellence with almost everything you do, you'll radically decrease the amount of pressure you put on yourself. After you eliminate the road-block of perfectionism, you'll experience far more success in all of your health behaviors.

TODAY

- Do something less than perfectly. Don't make your bed. Leave a few crumbs on the kitchen counters. Hang a picture at a crooked angle and leave it that way all day.

- Eat one food that's not on your current diet plan. Even one chocolate chip can help you realize you don't lose ground just because you took one step off the side of the road.

- Record your imperfection in your notebook. Add a few lines about how it felt to do this exercise.

❊ DAY 74 ❊
Watch for rainbows

Do you ever have days when absolutely everything seems to go wrong? Maybe it's rainy and cold outside, you got to work late, and your kids are fighting again. Pretty soon everything around you feels bleak and discouraging. During times like this, food begins to look like a really good friend.

But wait! You certainly don't have to give in and eat. Don't let these challenges or discouragements affect your weight-loss actions. Instead of letting your struggles pull you down, start training yourself to notice all the good things around you.

Watch for the unexpected

Sometimes the best things in life are totally unexpected. To get back your joy and sunshine, watch for the positive things that show up when you aren't even looking for them.

Label these tiny bright spots as *rainbows*—gifts that slip in quietly, giving you an emotional boost right in the middle of an otherwise difficult day.

Many times the world steps in and takes care of you without requiring anything in return. In order to take advantage of these unexpected treats, you have to open your heart and notice when they appear in your life.

Look around you. Is the sun shining? Was someone kind to you at the bank or in the grocery store? Did you drink a great cup of tea this afternoon? While these may seem like small things, if you pay attention to your rainbows and appreciate them, you can totally change your outlook.

Rainbows are everywhere

Sometimes noticing rainbows involves being grateful for what's already there. For example, do you have at least one person who truly loves and accepts you? Did you recently finish reading an inspirational book or a great newspaper article? Perhaps a song on the radio tugged at your emotions or brightened your spirit.

Cultivate a sense of gratitude for the simple things that happen in your life. Be thankful each time your children arrive home safely after school. At bedtime, appreciate your cozy blanket and the way your pillow fluffs up under your head. Make notes about your rainbows and consider all the ways they help you feel better.

TODAY

- Open your eyes wider and notice all the positive things that happen around you. Watch for bits of joy, kindness, and beauty that cross your path. Keep your notebook handy and record all of these rainbows as they show up.

- At the end of your day, tell yourself, "This was a really good day because . . ." and then read your list. As you recall each rainbow, remind yourself of the pleasure and comfort it brought you.

- During the weeks ahead, continue to watch for more tiny rainbows to smile about, then celebrate and appreciate every one of them.

❧ DAY 75 ❧
Small wins

Janet sighed deeply. "Yesterday was just another wasted day on my diet plan. I ate too much and I didn't exercise. I yelled at the kids and burned the dinner. Lately every day seems to go the same way—I have good intentions, but most of the time, I don't stick with my plans."

I prodded her gently. "Tell me about the rest of your day." Janet thought for a minute and then said, "Well, I cooked oatmeal for my son, who loves it. While I was at the store, I listened to an employee who felt depressed. And oh yes, I drank four glasses of water by noon."

Janet stopped briefly, and then she continued, "I also called my husband to see how his stressful meeting went. Then I wrote an outline for my church women's class. And before dinner I trimmed off the overcooked areas of the casserole so my family wouldn't have to eat them."

"Wait a minute," I interrupted. "I'm amazed to hear what a caring, successful day you had. A minute ago, you gave an entire list of things that went wrong. Where are they now?" Janet quietly admitted, "I can't remember any of them!"

Notice small wins

Yesterday you learned to watch for all the rainbows that pop up in your day. Now look at your *own actions* and identify all the ones that help move you closer to your goals. Label these as *small wins*. These include any of your efforts that make you feel more successful, happy, healthy, or peaceful.

Maybe you took a few minutes to play with your child, call a close friend, or commend a fellow employee. Perhaps you drank lots of water, smiled at a stranger, or gave yourself a fresh manicure. Even taking a hot, relaxing bath instead of going to bed feeling tense can be counted as a small win.

In your efforts to follow a healthy lifestyle, even the smallest steps count. Eating your vegetables or fruit, climbing stairs instead of taking the elevator, all of these are small wins.

Affirm your success

Watch for times when you have small wins, then write them down or mentally note what happened. Stack these wins on top of each other and then look for ways to create more of them.

As you affirm your small wins, the slipups in your day will seem a lot less important. And by focusing on your accomplishments, you'll always end the day feeling like a success instead of a failure.

TODAY

- Write down at least five things you did today that were small wins.

- Before you go to bed, read your list out loud and tell yourself you are a great success!

- Keep doing this for at least a week, perhaps even for a few months. Read your list each night and notice how it affects your attitude.

☙ DAY 76 ❧
Emotional safety

If you're like most people, you carefully protect yourself and your physical safety. You buckle up when you get into the car, lock your doors at night, and stay out of the scary parts of town. But how do you take care of your *emotional* safety?

When you feel unsettled, anxious, and insecure, you need a way to regroup and feel safe again. *Emotional safety* gives you a sense of being "grounded" as well as protected, strong, and secure. When you feel emotionally safe, you can relax, heave a big sigh, and say, "ahh . . ."—acknowledging that, at least for the moment, you are completely at ease.

Create a safe place

Think about how you can create an emotionally safe place in your life. Choose a room, a corner, or even a small area of a work cubicle that you can turn into your "ahh" space.

Gather a few favorite objects that always help you feel comfortable and secure. Personalize the area with posters, candles, or stuffed animals. Brighten it with flowers or plants and then add a CD player or a radio for soft, relaxing music.

Anytime life wears you down and leaves you feeling uneasy or discouraged, go to this "ahh" place and rebuild a sense of safety and calm. At work, renew your energy and your focus by touching the objects in your "ahh" corner.

Don't ignore your need for emotional safety. Instead, notice when you feel anxious or unsettled, then intentionally do something that will help you feel grounded and solid again.

Instant emotional safety

With a few simple actions, you can create some emotional safety anywhere. For example, if you go to a lot of meetings, carry your favorite coffee cup or a special notebook with you. This will give you something familiar to hold on to, especially during tense discussions. After a hard day at work, ease your tension on the way home by listening to a CD of your favorite upbeat music.

When you go through major changes such as starting a new job or moving to a different home, don't wait for months to "fix things up." Instead, focus on creating your "ahh" spaces immediately. Seek out an area that you can use as an oasis or a safe retreat, even in the midst of chaos. The bathtub, a nearby park, your car, even a neighborhood coffee shop can all be turned into safe places where you can regroup when you need to.

TODAY

- Decide where you can create an "ahh" place for yourself. A corner of a room or even an overstuffed chair with a cozy blanket can do the trick.

- Personalize this area with a variety of nurturing items such as plants, photos, or stuffed animals.

- Sit in the safe place you've created, then pull out your journal and describe your setting, including how you feel when you are in it.

✿ DAY 77 ✿
The healing power of rituals

Another way to build emotional safety is to create habits or rituals that help you feel more settled. Rituals include any specifically designed patterns or series of activities that serve a purpose such as helping you relax or reenergize.

Rituals help you feel emotionally safe because they allow you to draw on familiar things and activities rather than constantly having to think up new ones.

Look at the rituals or patterns you already have in place. For example, at your work, do you start the day by getting a hot cup of coffee, then making the rounds and greeting your friends? When you get home, do you typically sit down and read the mail before planning your evening?

Healing rituals

Think about your current rituals and notice how many of them involve food. You may need to replace some of these with healthier patterns for times when you want to relieve stress, calm down, or heal your emotional needs.

If you tend to head for the cupboard after a bad day, catch yourself and instead do a healing or relaxing ritual that will manage your stress or frustration in a better way.

One of my favorite healing rituals involves having tea. First, I make a pot of tea and place it on the table next to a blue cushioned chair in my living room. Then with soothing piano music in the background, I sip tea from a special china cup while I read a book or a recent magazine. It always works!

Here are some ideas for healing rituals:

- Sit quietly and listen to a specific song or type of music, such as a favorite classical piece.

- Light candles and meditate or sit in silence for a while before making dinner.

- Read a few pages from a special book such as the Bible, a novel, or a collection of poetry.

- Have a cup of tea or coffee along with a healthy snack.

- Listen to quiet instrumental music at night before you drift off to sleep.

When you travel, plan ways you can feel more at home in a hotel room or someone else's house. Tuck your favorite slippers into your suitcase and bring some photos of your loved ones to place on a bedside stand. Bring along a few packets of your favorite gourmet tea.

TODAY

- Create a ritual or pattern you can use any time you need to feel more settled or relaxed.

- In your notebook, describe what you'll do, where you'll do it, and what items you'll include in this special time. Maybe your ritual involves having your morning cup of coffee by a sunny window or creating a special romantic dinner.

- At some point today, use a ritual that helps you feel nurtured, calmed, or energized.

❧ DAY 78 ❧

Ditch the critic

Do you ever try to motivate yourself by being critical or by using negative self-talk? Unfortunately, punishing yourself doesn't usually cause you to change your behavior. Instead your brain hears your negative, chastising thoughts, and then it attempts to make them true. In fact, whenever you label yourself with words such as *failure*, you usually just drag yourself down further.

It's time for you to ditch the critic inside your head and take the opposite approach. Start telling yourself, "Come on, you're truly capable of doing anything!" These positive messages will help you feel more inspired to stay with your goals.

Speak kindly!

The type or amount of food you eat does not determine your self-worth! So remind yourself that even on days when you gobble down a bag of chips or devour a huge piece of cake, you are still a good person.

Pretend for a minute that you're talking with a small child. Now picture yourself sitting on the floor and gently saying, "The fact that you ate candy before dinner or broke your toy doesn't change who you are. You are still a valuable person regardless of what you did."

Start treating yourself with the same level of tenderness and respect as you would that child. If you slip up on your goals, don't beat yourself up for being a "failure." Instead, hold your head up high and tell yourself, "I'm important, I'm valuable, and I count in this world."

I'm still worthwhile!

Jack Canfield, coauthor of the *Chicken Soup for the Soul* series, teaches a great way to change negative self-talk. He encourages workshop participants to respond to "put-downs" or negative messages by saying, *"No matter what you say or do to me, I am still a worthwhile person!"*

Saying this phrase again and again will help you mentally contradict hurtful or cut-down comments that can harm your self-esteem. It will also help you stop the negative messages inside your own head.

During times when you don't finish the work project on time or your spouse yells at you because you forgot to pick up the dry cleaning, just pull out the "I'm still a worthwhile person" phrase and repeat it to yourself as many times as necessary. Then live as if it were true—because it is!

TODAY

- In your notebook, write down, "No matter what you say or do to me, I am still a worthwhile person."

- Then underline or highlight the words so they really hit home.

- Say this to yourself at least a dozen times today. Anytime you hear negative things from other people as well as from yourself, repeat this phrase.

❦ DAY 79 ❦

Live as a "healthy" person

You're tired of salads and you're bored with grilled chicken breast. When you've been on a diet for a while, you may begin longing for a little more variety and fun in your plan. All you really want is to be able to eat like a "normal" person.

But in reality, this may not be quite what you had in mind. Stop and think about it. Most of the "normal" people in our society *eat way too much, make poor food choices, and don't care.* Is that what you're striving for?

Think *healthy* instead of *thin*

When you talk about your weight-loss efforts, begin changing your words to match your lifestyle goals. Maybe you always tell yourself that you want to be *thin* or *skinny*. Rather than using these vague, weight-related words, describe your goal as part of a long-term plan that includes other aspects of life. Instead of aiming to be thin, consider using words such as *healthy, fit, active, balanced,* or *strong.*

In fact, start creating a new image of how you will live as a "healthy" person. What does a healthy person do each day? What type of eating and exercise programs do healthy people follow? And what attitudes do healthy people have toward food, eating, exercise, and coping with life?

This new wording may change how you think about a lot of things. For instance, over the long run, a fit or strong person will probably sustain a much healthier lifestyle than a thin per-

172

son. The difference is that now these are lifetime goals, not just ones related to staying on a diet plan.

Encourage children to be healthy

You can also teach children to use these new labels. Instead of setting goals around losing weight or getting thin, you can encourage children to improve their levels of health, fitness, strength, or other physical and emotional qualities.

When you discuss eating plans with your kids, avoid using words such as *dieting* or *weight loss*. Instead, refer to *healthy food plans, better nutrition,* and *being physically fit*. If you talk about their weight, use words such as *healthy* or *active*. For example, say, "We want to eat in ways that will make us healthier." Or you might say, "Let's take a walk to improve how fit and strong we are."

TODAY

- In the center of a page in your notebook, draw a stick figure or other image of yourself. Beneath the picture, write the words "A Healthy _____" and fill in your first name.

- Draw lines outward from the picture, and then label each one with an area of your life, such as eating, exercise, relationships or family, work, and fun.

- Describe how you will work on each of these areas as a healthy person, not as a *thin* or *skinny* one.

❧ DAY 80 ❧

Get a new title

When you struggle with your eating or with gaining weight, you might be tempted to describe yourself with words such as *fat, lazy, failure,* or *screw-up.* Unfortunately, when you create a negative view of yourself, you will usually match it by how you live.

For example, if you hold a primary image of yourself as a "fat slob," you'll probably continue to live like one. In the same way, if you attempt to motivate yourself by using a "fat" photo or a picture of a pig, it usually backfires.

You see, your brain doesn't recognize the difference between a negative image and a positive one, and it may assume that you actually want to look like the pig.

Use positive words

To change the way you see yourself, you may have to create a different picture. I'm not suggesting that you pretend you're thin when you aren't. But using more positive language will help you focus on your potential instead of your mistakes. Rather than seeing yourself as a failure, create new images of yourself moving forward and making progress.

In his book *The 3-Hour Diet,* Jorge Cruise recommends that you create a new *name tag* or something special to call yourself. Come up with a positive, happy one that moves you toward your goals. He says, "Use a very descriptive name such as 'sexy mama' or 'hot babe' or 'power woman,' then live in ways that make the title real for you."

Your new description

In addition to your new title, pick out a word or phrase that describes yourself without referring to your weight or your size. Use this descriptive word any time you are deciding how to manage your life challenges.

For example, Cheryl liked the word *fit* much better than the word *thin*, so she used that as her description. Now, when she's at a party or dealing with a stressful day, she asks herself, "How would a *fit* Cheryl handle this?"

TODAY

- Choose a word or a phrase for describing yourself. Pick one you'll be comfortable with for many years. Avoid using words such as *thin, svelte,* or *skinny.* Instead, choose from ones such as *balanced, fit, healthy, strong,* and *solid.*

- In your notebook, write down the phrase "I am a _____ (healthy, fit, etc.) person" and then fill in your new word.

- Describe your daily life by saying, "This is what a _____ (healthy, fit, etc.) person does."

DAYS 71–80 COMPLETED!

You've come this far in your 100 days . . .

Don't stop now. If you're struggling to stick with it, push yourself to finish *one more day.* You'll immediately be another day closer to achieving your weight-loss goals.

Just do one more day!

❧ DAYS 81–90 ❧

☘ DAY 81 ☘
Unhook the chains

It always starts with just one little thing. Maybe your child is sick or your washing machine quits working. When you walk into the kitchen, you're attacked by leftover brownies so you eat several of them. Later on, you feel exhausted from your day as well as frustrated because you overate. So to get it all out of your system, you finish off the evening by eating a large bowl of ice cream.

While these things may seem like a series of random events, they became connected until they wore down your resistance to food. In a *behavior chain,* one thing leads to another, increasing your frustration until you throw your hands up in the air and reach for the cookies or the M&M's.

Struggles with emotional eating rarely happen in isolation. If your finances are already stretched, the broken washing machine simply adds another layer to your anxiety. And on days when you're operating by a thread, seeing an open pizza box can be too much for your fragile willpower.

Ask, "And what else?"

To examine the links in a behavior chain, start by identifying the exact time you first ate or knew you desperately wanted to eat. Working backward from there, ask yourself, "What happened? What bothered me or made me upset?"

Then consider all of the situations or people that may have prompted your stressful feelings or other emotions. As you identify items along the way, keep asking *"And what else?"* to jog your memory about other issues that affected you.

Study the links

After you identify all the links in an eating-related chain of events, look carefully at each one. Determine exactly which places you slipped up and consider what you could have done to prevent them. For example, did you get way too hungry? Were you trying to keep yourself from exploding at your boss or your children? Maybe you skipped your regular lunchtime walk that always helps you manage your stress.

Rather than focus on how much you ate, think about other ways you could have handled the problems in your day. By stopping the sequence at the third event instead of waiting until the tenth one, you may be able to prevent yourself from heading for the cupboard.

TODAY

- In your notebook, draw a behavior chain of events you experienced today or during a recent week.

- Keep asking "And what else?" Then add more items to the list until you've exhausted all the possible links in the chain.

- With each link, write a note about any actions you could have taken to handle the problem instead of letting it build.

☙ DAY 82 ☙
Last-straw eating

After one more thing happens on an already stressful day, it's easy to exclaim, "That was the last straw!" and then head for the kitchen to dive into the bag of cookies. Although it may seem as if it was the *last straw* that prompted you to give in and eat, you probably began to weaken much earlier.

Recognize the chain

When Jill ate five pieces of pizza at the mall one night, she assumed it was because she was overly tired from shopping. But as she looked at the events and emotions from earlier in the day, it was obvious that fatigue wasn't the only problem.

By asking "And what else?" Jill was able to identify a series of events and issues that contributed to her eating. Here is her "behavior chain" of events:

- I was awfully tired from shopping, and the food court was a convenient place to rest.

- I really didn't want to go to the mall but my daughter begged me to go.

- My husband and I were supposed to go to dinner with friends but we couldn't get a babysitter.

- I was irritated because my husband was supposed to call the babysitter and he forgot.

- My husband went to dinner with our friends anyway, so I felt disappointed and left out.

- Instead of coming home before dinner, he worked late, then went directly to the restaurant.

- I was missing him a lot and I wished that he'd stopped at home first.

- I guess it's all connected to his phone call earlier in the day. He said they just announced some more layoffs at his company and this time, his job may be at risk.

The "last straw" started earlier

Jill probably *did* eat because she was so tired. But while her fatigue was the "last straw," the real source of her emotional eating could be found earlier on the list. In addition to her anger and frustration about the dinner party, Jill was feeling anxious and fearful about her husband's job.

TODAY

- Watch for events that hook together, putting you at risk for "last-straw eating." For example, your mom calls, your kitchen's a mess, your husband is working late again, the washing machine makes a bad noise, and so on.

- Think of ways you can prevent last-straw eating. Plan at least one thing that will protect you from eating when you reach that frustration point.

- In your notebook, write down one action you can always reach for on days when a series of events wears you down. Maybe even a few deep breaths can stop the behavior chain from sending you to the refrigerator.

⚜ DAY 83 ⚜

No more deprivation

Suppose you host a birthday party where everyone else has ice cream and cake while you just drink black coffee. You really want to stay on your diet, but watching everyone eat 'makes you feel deprived and left out. So after your guests have gone home, you sneak into the kitchen and eat three pieces of leftover cake. After all, you deserve to have a little fun too, don't you?

Do you sometimes give in and eat because you feel *deprived?* But stop and think about the whole concept of deprivation. Is it really such a horrible thing? And does it always have to push you off your diet path? Like it or not, to successfully manage your weight, you have to set boundaries around your eating. And even if it makes you feel deprived, sometimes you may have to turn down a wonderful piece of cake.

Life includes deprivation

In your daily life, deprivation happens everywhere. In fact, you deprive yourself of a lot of things because you'd rather have the *benefits* you get as a result. For example, because you prefer getting a paycheck, you sacrifice spending your days skiing or playing at the beach. And if you value keeping your marriage, you probably deprive yourself of going on dates.

In the same way, depriving yourself of dessert might mean that you're able to successfully manage your weight. When you feel deprived in regard to food, look at the benefits you're getting as a result of your actions. Then decide what's more important—losing weight or experiencing the brief pleasure of eating a piece of chocolate cake.

Weight deprives you, too

If you can't get past your struggle with feeling deprived, try switching it around by asking: *"What does my weight deprive me of?"* Then make a list of the things you're missing out on by being overweight.

For example, are there life experiences or adventures that you generally have to skip? Is your size preventing you from achieving some of your dreams and goals? What about the toll on your confidence and your self-esteem? Rather than dwelling on how deprived you feel because you can't have a piece of chocolate cake, work on improving your life and your health so you can enjoy all the things you're missing.

TODAY

- In your journal, write about "poor me." Talk about any situations in which you feel deprived, abused, or singled out because of your dieting efforts.

- Now reverse the question and ask: "What does my weight deprive me of?" Make a list of all the things you miss out on because of your weight.

- Measure this list against the times you might feel deprived around food, and then decide you'll work on changing your life so you can begin to enjoy things you're currently missing.

❧ DAY 84 ❧

The expectation square

With almost everything in life, you hold a mental picture of how things *should* be. For example, you expect that a restaurant will have clean tables, an attentive wait staff, and good food. Think of this picture as your *expectation square*, sort of a mental snapshot of how it's supposed to be.

You create expectation squares for everything, from how you expect your kids to behave to how you want to be treated by your boss. But if your expectations tend to be rigid or unbending, you can end up with mental squares that are very small.

Typical
expectation
square

Rigid
expectation
square

The tighter or more rigid your squares are, the less likely the world will match them. People or things are almost never as they *should* be, so you can get frustrated because life doesn't match what you want. These unmet expectations will often contribute to your struggles with food and eating.

Widen the square

If real life never seems to match your picture, you may need to change your image of what you consider acceptable. In other words, you need to *widen your square*. You can do this with your own behavior as well as with what you expect from others.

Allow it to be different

In order to widen your expectation square, you have to be willing to allow things to be different than you'd like. Start by creating a different version of your expectation. Fill in the square with your new picture and then ask yourself: *"Could it be like this and still be okay?"*

Imagine all the places where you could apply this concept. Suppose your child brings home a disappointing report card. What if the person in the grocery line in front of you has 12 items instead of 10? How do you react when your overworked boss snaps at you? In each of these situations, widening your expectation square will give you a much calmer reaction. It may also prevent you from reaching for a cookie to handle your frustration.

TODAY

- In your notebook, draw a small square to show an area of your life and then describe where you have a rigid view of how it "should" be.

- Next, draw a larger square around it. Then write down ways you could widen your expectations and allow other options.

- Do this with several other areas that frustrate you in life. With each larger square you draw, ask the question: "Could it be like this and still be okay?"

❧ DAY 85 ❧

Let it go

You worked at widening your square and becoming more accepting. But you're certainly not happy about it. At times you may wonder, "Why do I always have to be the one who gives in? *It's not fair!*"

You're right. A lot of things are not fair. But bitterness and resentment will simply allow your negative feelings such as anger and frustration to keep eating at you. After a while, instead of resolving your emotions and moving past them, you carry them around like a huge rock on your shoulders.

When others have emotionally hurt you, it's easy to say, "They can't treat me this way! I'll make them pay!" But somehow, these other people never seem to suffer very much. In your efforts to "show them," you're the one who overeats, gains weight, or feels depressed.

Let them go

Learn how to set a time limit on your feelings, and then let them go. To do this, choose a difficult situation and write down or mentally list all your thoughts and emotions about it. Then either on a piece of paper or mentally, place all of these thoughts into the palm of your hand.

Decide how long you want to hold on to these emotions. Pick a time limit, using anywhere from a few seconds to several hours. Close your fist tightly around the feelings and hold them until the time is up. At the end of the time limit, open your hand

and throw the paper away or mentally send those thoughts into outer space.

As you let the feelings go, stretch your arm to its full length and hold your hand open with the palm facing up. Mentally picture those negative emotions flowing down your arm and out through your fingers, then watch all of them drift away.

Repeat as necessary

When you release a feeling, make sure you completely let go of it. Don't pick it up again or allow it to creep back into your thoughts. If you can't seem to get rid of a bad feeling, repeat the process of setting a time limit. Once again, decide how long you will hold on to that emotion, and when the time is up, let it go.

TODAY

- Choose a specific item, person, or situation that makes you feel angry, frustrated, hurt, or sad. In your notebook, describe this in detail.

- Mentally or with a piece of paper, place this issue into the palm of your hand. Hold it for a specific length of time, and then let it go. If necessary, do this several times in order to release the feelings.

- In your notebook, write a few lines that affirm you've let go of the issue as well as the feelings around it.

⚜ DAY 86 ⚜

Minimize the damage

In going through this 100 Days Program, you've learned a lot of new tricks and skills for managing your weight. But many times, real life will get in the way of your plans. Besides your emotional issues, things such as out-of-town visitors, work parties, or even a cruise can challenge your efforts.

Before you know it, you're back digging into the brownies or cheesecake or lasagna. Soon your overeating screws your diet up so much that you wonder if you should quit your program entirely, at least for now. But wait—you don't have to give up just because of a little extra eating.

If you leave your children with a babysitter, you don't forget you have kids. In the same way, going off your diet doesn't mean you can forget you have one. Instead of giving up when you're faced with difficult times, stay on your plan by using the simple phrase, *"Minimize the damage!"*

Stop while it's small

Although advertising proclaims "you can't eat just one," you don't have to believe this line. Build a strong confidence that you can stop eating and get back on track. Even when you really slip up on your plan, you can still reach for your skills and decrease the amount of damage you allow to happen.

When you have one of those times when you can't seem to resist temptation, pull out any tools that will help you get back in control—sit on your hands, leave the room, brush your teeth, or even throw out the rest of the food. By taking action right away, you can stop a few bites from becoming a binge.

At family dinners, create your own system to minimize the damage. Do the same thing for times when you get caught by work parties, unplanned events, or drop-in visitors. Keep a list of your best tricks such as focusing on the first two bites and postponing eating. If you feel weak and you're about to give in to a food trigger, leave the setting and shift your focus to something other than food.

Use the tasting diet

On a cruise or a vacation, consider using the idea of being on a *tasting diet*. You can still experiment with trying out new foods or enjoying desserts. But with anything that isn't part of your fuel needs for the day, have just a taste or limit yourself to only two bites. Savor the food, appreciate all the flavors, then get away from the table and do something else.

TODAY

- Think about any high-risk activities or possible food temptations that you'll be facing during the next few weeks.

- Try to come up with at least three ways that you can minimize the damage in these situations.

- Record your plan in your notebook, and then read it often during the next few days so that you'll feel strong and prepared.

☀ DAY 87 ☀

Old habits

Right now you may feel totally confident that *this time* you will never gain back your weight. I certainly hope you're right. But unfortunately you still have to deal with the same family members, bad weather, and work issues that always hurt your enthusiasm in the past. Plus, a few of your old habits probably haven't completely disappeared, and some of them may look appealing again very soon.

Get rid of old habits

Almost without exception, people who regain weight admit it's because they *slipped back into their old habits*. It starts out with skipping your usual oatmeal one morning, then having a doughnut and coffee on the way to work.

Just a few days later, you remember how good that doughnut tasted, so you stop at the coffee shop again. Before long, you slip back into your old habit of eating a couple of doughnuts every morning before you go to work.

Sometimes you simply let a routine slip away. Maybe you miss a day or two on your exercise program, and now it seems easier to grab a bag of chips than to walk on your treadmill. Perhaps you return to the solace of a bowl of ice cream before bedtime. Or you go back to eating in the car instead of taking time to sit down and relax with your meal.

To prevent slipping back into your old habits, you may still have to break the patterns that got you into them in the first place. Begin with identifying times when you eat strictly out of habit, then decide how you could change your routine.

Create new patterns

If you have certain times you always associate with food, look for ways to shake things up. For example, instead of heading straight for the kitchen when you get home from work, try doing something that will break your normal pattern. Turn into your driveway from the opposite side or use the back door of your home instead of your usual entrance.

If you always search through the refrigerator before you get ready for bed, go back to relaxing with a warm bath. When you sit down to watch a TV football game, switch from drinking beer to having a diet soda.

With family rituals such as eating ice cream or pizza together, figure out how to stop yourself from automatically joining in. You might need to invent some new ways to feel connected, even if you're the only person in the group who changes.

TODAY

- In your notebook, make a list of habits that have caused you trouble in the past.

- Don't forget the can of nuts or the candy bars you used to hide in your drawer at work. What about the fried cheese sticks or barbecued chicken wings you always ate at happy hour?

- Write a few sentences about how you can avoid slipping back into those old habits.

❧ DAY 88 ❧
I do care!

If you're like most people, you get tired of staying on your diet, pushing yourself to exercise, and avoiding all the fun times around food. Sometimes you may get so discouraged that you decide you just don't care anymore. When you get worn down, it's tempting to let up on your dieting efforts or even to give up entirely.

Don't stop caring!

In our lives, we tend to want whatever's easy. And eating is definitely easy. But to stop your pattern of reaching for food as a quick fix, you have to stick with your diet even during times when you don't feel like it. On a bad day when you're tempted to "not care," remind yourself that you are worth it and you deserve to improve your life and your health.

Paul was very determined to stay on his diet plan and reach his goal. Most days he felt strong with his program, but once in a while, he got discouraged and stopped caring.

One day he told me, "During lunch I went to the bakery and came back to my office with a big piece of chocolate cake. And was it ever good! But now I wish I had cared a little more before I gave in and ate it."

After his chocolate cake episode, Paul vowed that he wouldn't stop caring, no matter what. So he put a note on his computer screen where he would see it as soon as he got to work. Every morning he began his day by reading this: "I do care! I will always care! And I will make it!"

Figure out what's bothering you

In most cases when you don't feel like sticking with your diet plan, it's not that you don't care. It's more likely a sign that something else requires your attention. Maybe other things in life are demanding your energy or your focus.

When you're tempted to stop caring, dig past your excuses to see what might be getting to you. Rather than just giving up and deciding you don't care about your goals, take care of the real issues that are getting in your way.

TODAY

- Make a sign that says, "I do care!" Place it where you can see it easily, such as on your refrigerator, mirror, or computer screen.

- Remind yourself at least a dozen times today that deep down, you actually *do* care—no matter how difficult the day has been.

- Write down a few lines in your notebook to help you remember how much you care.

☙ DAY 89 ☙

At my best

How do you act when you're living and performing at your best? When life is going great, what kinds of things are in place for you? What gives you energy or makes you happy?

Remember the days when you felt confident, strong, capable, and able to face challenges head-on. Even if it's been years ago, think of times when you were truly *at your best* in many areas of your life, including physically as well as mentally and emotionally. Recall any times in the past when you were at a healthy weight or were exercising regularly.

"I used to be great!"

We never really lose our characteristics from the past. But as the years go by, we tend to lose sight of our strengths and our gifts. Sometimes we see only the parts of ourselves that we don't like. To bring back the qualities and concepts you've lost, remind yourself that you still value them. Then intentionally put them into your life again.

Today you'll build a list of words and phrases that describe what you are really like when you're at your absolute best. As you create your list, think of your best personality traits as well as your skills. Remember that all of these beautiful words remain true even on days when you don't feel like them.

What follows is an "at my best" list from Rita, a weight-loss client. She said, "Whenever I start feeling down about myself, I review my list. Then I try to live exactly like those descriptive phrases. It always pulls me back out of the dumps and helps me avoid using food to cheer myself up."

At my best, this is what I'm like:

- Energetic, bouncy, smile a lot, have twinkly eyes
- Laugh easily, tell jokes and funny stories
- Grounded, centered, confident about my abilities
- Productive, hard-working, accomplish a lot
- Blend well with people, relate easily, enjoy being with my friends
- Hug and cuddle my husband often, encourage sex and intimacy
- Connected spiritually, cultivate my faith, attend church regularly
- Physically strong, fit, flexible, play tennis and golf

TODAY

- In your notebook, write, "At my best, this is what I'm like:" Then list every descriptive word and phrase you can think of that portrays how you act, look, feel, or live when you are at your very best.

- Read your list *out loud* and notice the energy and enthusiasm it generates.

- Save your list and read it often, especially at times when your self-esteem droops. Remind yourself that all of these phrases are true, regardless of whether or not you feel that way.

※ DAY 90 ※
Live "as if"

Researchers have long known that if we pretend a little, eventually we can build a whole new pattern of behavior. In other words, by acting *as if* you have a particular skill or feeling, you can get past your fear and make that goal become real. For example, novice public speakers are trained to act *as if* they feel totally confident and they have no stage fright whatsoever. After pretending this a few times, most speakers find it becomes true.

Act as if it's real

In a study conducted many years ago, two groups of people who were depressed began taking regular walks as part of an experiment. The people in one group were simply told to walk for 20 minutes each day.

The other participants were told the same thing, but with one added instruction. Regardless of how they felt, they were told to hold their heads high and walk with a spirited step as if they felt great.

When the study was evaluated, the researchers found that nearly all of the participants from the "as if" group reported a significant improvement in their levels of depression and hopelessness. By acting *as if* they felt better, they did!

In the same way, you don't have to wait until *some day* when you've lost weight or found a new job to live at your best. When you get dressed each morning, look in the mirror and say, "I look great!" Then walk and talk *as if* you do.

Match your image

Think about how you would speak to others, do your work projects, and raise your children if you truly felt great about yourself. Then go through your days living as if you really do feel that way.

This approach doesn't mean you should put your head in the sand and ignore the realities of your life. It simply helps you develop a fresh attitude about what's already there. It also gives you hope that things can improve.

Here's a way to use this concept with your weight-loss efforts. Live *as if* you are totally able to manage your weight. After a month or so of acting as if you feel completely confident about following your diet and exercise plans, you'll be amazed at how well you'll begin to match this image.

TODAY

- Pick one item from the "at my best" list you wrote yesterday.

- All day long, act *as if* that one thing were true. For example, if you say that at your best you are funny and you laugh a lot, cultivate these traits by acting that way even if you don't feel like it.

- At the end of the day, notice how your outlook has changed. In your journal, write a few notes that describe how this approach worked for you.

DAYS 81–90 COMPLETED!

You've come this far in your 100 days . . .

Don't stop now. If you're struggling to stick with it, push yourself to finish *one more day.* You'll immediately be another day closer to achieving your weight-loss goals.

Just do one more day!

❦ DAYS 91–100 ❦

PUT IT INTO ACTION

DAY 91   Obesity is a condition

DAY 92   Accept the solution

DAY 93   20-year plan

DAY 94   Three columns of weight loss

DAY 95   Set your intentions

DAY 96   What will it take?

DAY 97   Use what works

DAY 98   New Year's resolution

DAY 99   It's not in here!

DAY 100   This is how I live!

※ DAY 91 ※

Obesity is a condition

If you're like most dieters, you can't wait for your program to be done. You keep hoping that one of these days you'll reach your goal weight and not have to think about it again. Unfortunately, this probably won't ever happen. Regardless of all the magazine promises and "after" photos, there is no such thing as *permanent* weight loss.

In reality, obesity is a *condition* just like diabetes. When people become diabetic, they have to learn how to get their condition under control, and then they have to live every day of their lives in a way that keeps it managed.

A diabetic can't leave town and proclaim, "Hooray! I'm now on vacation. I don't want to think about a thing, so I'll just leave my insulin at home!" For most diabetics, this would be a total disaster! Even after managing it for years, diabetics have to monitor their condition daily, including during vacations.

Manage your condition

Similar to the challenges of a diabetic, you can't ignore the condition of obesity. Once you have it, you're stuck. You are never completely free of this condition, and since it can't be cured, there's no being "done" with it.

Whether you've struggled with losing 10 pounds or more than 100 pounds, this condition stays with you forever. Even after you've reached your weight-loss goal, you are never finished. And no matter how consistent you are with your eating and your exercise efforts, for the rest of your life, you'll remain vulnerable to gaining your weight back.

Accept the condition

Don't let this scare you—it's completely possible to maintain your weight successfully for the long run. But in order to do this, you have to take care of your condition every day, in spite of vacations, holidays, job changes, and other life challenges.

If this concept feels uncomfortable, start by thinking in terms of *accepting* that you have a condition. You may have to work through some anger or frustration to reach this point. It's not easy to give up the myth of being "done" with managing your weight. But until you decide to accept this and live in a way that shows it, you risk gaining your weight back time and time again.

Think about what it might take to manage your condition in future years. Since you can't leave it home during social events or vacations, plan how you can manage your condition even when you're "out." As you continue to build these skills into your daily life, you'll have discovered one of the greatest secrets to long-term success.

TODAY

- How does it feel to have the *condition* of obesity? Do you resent this or think you'll simply ignore it?

- In your journal, write a paragraph or two about your condition and your plan for accepting the fact that you have it.

- Describe what you will do today to manage your ongoing condition.

❦ DAY 92 ❦

Accept the solution

L et's suppose that even though you're not happy about it, you've decided to accept that *obesity is a condition* and that you're stuck with it long-term.

Now it's time to add one more piece—you have to be willing to *accept the solution*. That means you not only have to live in a way that matches your goals at the moment, you also have to accept that you'll be doing this for the rest of your life.

What's your plan?

It seems so unfair. Why is it that some people can eat all they want and never gain an ounce? Who knows? There's simply no easy answer to that question. What counts is that you are choosing to manage your weight long-term, regardless of how others around you are living.

During the past 100 days, maybe you've made a lot of progress but you still want to lose more weight. Perhaps you've reached your goal and you're determined to maintain your success. Either way, you still have to accept the solution for managing your weight forever. And for some people, this is even harder than accepting the condition.

Look at it this way—
A decision about what to weigh is a decision about how to live.

In other words, if you're committed to staying at your goal weight, you have to adopt the way of life that goes with it.

202

To manage your weight long-term, you'll always have to apply certain guidelines and boundaries to your food intake. That means you no longer have the option of supersizing your meals or eating everything you want.

It also means that you'll need to develop a realistic exercise program that works for all of the seasons. And when holidays roll around, you'll have to come up with a clear strategy to help you get through the mounds of mashed potatoes, candy, and pumpkin pie.

Even with making a clear decision about "how to live," you'll probably have days or even weeks when you'll let up on your efforts. But to be successful over the long run, you'll have to commit to always *accepting the solution.*

TODAY

- Think about your solutions for the condition of obesity. Are you willing to accept the changes you'll have to make in order to manage this for life?

- Write down your thoughts on how you feel about accepting the solution.

- Make a decision about what you want to weigh long-term and record it in your notebook. Add a few thoughts on how you can live in a way that supports that decision.

☆ DAY 93 ☆

20-year plan

Just as you brush your teeth or take a shower every day, you can also create a regular routine for managing your weight. Start with planning out your daily actions for the coming week, including how you'll eat, exercise, and take care of your emotional needs. Then turn this plan into a long-term blueprint that you can follow every day of your life.

My 20-year plan

To put this concept into a different perspective, think ahead to the next 20 years. What types of things can you see yourself doing consistently for 20 years or longer? With the following exercise, first determine your answers for each section, and then combine them into a lasting plan for daily life.

1. What I can do for the next 20 years

Make a list of seven items that you'll keep in your eating plan for the next 20 years. Include ways you'll manage your food intake, make healthier choices, and handle life challenges around eating.

Rather than listing specific numbers of calories or points, you might want to use general guidelines, such as that you'll eat low-fat foods, monitor portions, and listen to your levels of hunger and fullness.

2. Favorite foods

Choose three of your favorite foods. Then using the concept of *smaller amounts, less often,* decide how you'll plan these foods into your program, not out of it.

3. Exercise

Decide on the amount of exercise you plan to do regularly. If you like, add a few goals that will help you become stronger or more physically fit. Then define your specific exercise plan as well as how you'll stick with it.

4. Barriers

Identify any potential barriers such as stress or emotional eating that might keep you from being able to maintain your success. List strategies for how you'll handle these problems so they won't sabotage your efforts.

5. Crisis management

Come up with an action plan you can use immediately if you begin gaining weight. Determine your "red flags," such as hitting a certain weight on the scale or not fitting into your favorite pair of jeans. Any time these red flags show up, set your crisis plan into motion.

TODAY

In your notebook, write the title "My 20-year Plan," and then create a blueprint for how you'll live for the next 20 years. Follow the specific directions in each of the sections above. Here's a quick summary:

- Seven things I can do forever

- Three favorite foods and a plan for managing them

- My exercise plan and how I'll make it work

- Barriers and life issues—a plan for handling them

- Immediate crisis plan if I begin gaining weight

☘ DAY 94 ☘

Three columns of weight loss

Every day, from the time you get up in the morning until you go to bed at night, you live out your day in one of three behavior columns—*weight loss, maintain,* or *gain.* With these categories, there's no gray or in-between. At the end of the day, you'll know exactly which one matched your life.

Weight-loss column

When you live in the weight-loss column, you stick with your diet and exercise plan all day. That doesn't necessarily mean that you follow it perfectly. But if every single day, you ate, exercised, and coped with life in the same way as you did on this one, you'd probably lose weight consistently.

Maintain column

In the maintain column, you don't necessarily go off your diet or your exercise plan. But at the same time, you're not completely solid with it either. Maybe you eat dessert or grab a few high-fat snacks or an extra slice of pizza. If every day matched this one, you might not lose any pounds, but you'd probably maintain your current weight.

Gain column

On days when you slip into the gain column, you might eat too much food or have more sweets and snacks than usual. You probably don't exercise either. And if you lived every day exactly the same way as this one, you'd most likely see your weight go back up.

90 percent rule

You can't stay on a diet plan only half of the time and expect to see results. To truly achieve long-term success, you have to live at least 90 percent of your days in either the *weight-loss* or the *maintain* column. This translates to nine out of ten days or, if you prefer, think of it as nine out of ten meals.

If you consistently spend more than 10 percent of the time in the gain column, you probably won't experience very much success with managing your weight. That means if you follow your diet plan during the week but eat whatever you want on the weekends, there's a good chance you'll end up gaining weight.

So pick your spot. Decide where you want to be, and then follow through with living in that column. Don't kid yourself and say that you're "trying" to lose weight. If you really want to accomplish your goal, stay in the column it requires.

TODAY

- Ask yourself, "If I lived every day exactly the same way as I did today, what would happen? Would I lose weight, maintain my weight, or gain weight?"

- Record your answer in your journal and then describe which actions (or lack of actions) determined your column for today.

- Consider tracking this over a number of weeks to see how close you come to the 90 percent rule.

❧ DAY 95 ❧

Set your intentions

Do you set goals but never follow through with achieving them? It's always easy to say, "I really want to lose 20 pounds" or "I've got to start exercising every day." But often these wonderful statements never turn into action. To become more effective with making these things happen, define your goals as *intentions* and clarify what you want to do.

Start with making your intentions measurable so you can tell if you've achieved them or not. For example, if you say, "Today I'm going to take a 20-minute walk," by this evening you should be able to report whether you walked or not.

Intention starts the action

To set an intention, first create a specific statement that tells what you want to do. Follow it with a plan that states exactly how you'll follow through with accomplishing this intention. For example, suppose you decide you want to stop eating ice cream every night before going to bed. Here's how you might lay out a plan for being successful with this goal.

MY ACTION PLAN FOR BEDTIME

Throw out the ice cream that's currently in the freezer and don't buy any more for a while. Purchase a new fiction book. After dinner, pull out my favorite herbal tea and get a nice mug out of the cupboard. Set these things on the table along with my book. At 9:30 p.m., put on my pajamas and make the tea. Sit in my blue chair while I drink tea and read for the next half hour, then go to bed.

When intentions don't happen

If you keep saying you want to accomplish something but you never do, look for the holes in your system. Evaluate whether you've placed any barriers in your way or if you're making it difficult to take action. Maybe you plan to get up an hour earlier to exercise, but you keep going to bed at the same late hour as always.

Think carefully about your intention. How important is this goal right now? Are you sure it's something that you really want to do? Do you need more time, money, or other resources to make it happen? If your intention just doesn't seem to be happening, maybe you need to simplify your plan or alter it to make it more realistic.

For example, if your intention is to exercise regularly, doing a 30-minute run might seem like a wonderful goal. But if you haven't been exercising at all, you'll probably have more success if you set an intention to walk for 20 minutes or jog a distance of three blocks.

TODAY

- Set a specific intention around achieving one of your weight-loss goals. Say "My intention is to . . ." and then write down what you want to accomplish.

- Plan your action steps and then add details that will make it easier to follow through with your plan.

- Create several more intentions, then record them in your notebook along with your action plans to make them happen.

❧ DAY 96 ❧
What will it take?

If you continue to struggle with following through on your goals, try breaking them down into smaller and smaller actions until you run out of excuses for not doing your plan.

What will it take?
After you create your first action step, ask: *"What will it take to make that happen?"* Once you figure this out, use your answer to spell out a new intention.

Each time you identify another action, ask yourself: "What will it take to make *that* happen?" Do this again and again until you reach an action you can't escape, no matter what. Label this final action as a *now* goal. Then get up from your chair and do it.

For example, suppose you decide you'll walk during your lunch break, but you keep forgetting to bring your walking shoes to work. Here's how you can use the principle of "What will it take?" to follow through with your intention.

By the way, you can abbreviate "What will it take?" with the letters WWT. Remember that each time you ask the question, your answer becomes your next intention.

What is my intention? Bring gym shoes to work.

WWT? Put them in the car when I get home.

What is my intention? Put shoes in the car this evening.

WWT? Stick a note on my briefcase to remind myself.

What is my intention? Write a note to remind myself.

WWT? Do it right now.

Break it into smaller parts

Setting intentions works for everything from tiny goals such as taking a walk, to bigger plans such as training to participate in a race. Just keep breaking your intentions into small steps that you can accomplish easily. With each new goal, ask yourself, "What will *that* take?" Then create an action plan for the next part of your goals.

Here's a simplified example for getting back on your exercise program. Notice how each time you ask, "What will *that* take?" your answer becomes the new intention.

WWT? Renew my membership at the health club; work with a personal trainer.

WWT? Stop at the club and sign up to meet with a trainer.

WWT? Plan an exercise session with the trainer into my schedule for sometime this week.

WWT? Pull out my schedule book and write the session into a day that works.

WWT? Do it now!

TODAY

- In your notebook, write down a goal or activity you want to accomplish.

- Create an action step by asking yourself: "What will that take?" (WWT)

- Repeat this sequence four or five times until you have an immediate action step, and then *do it*.

❧ DAY 97 ❧
Use what works

Think back to previous times when you've done well with losing weight or exercising regularly. Perhaps you had great success at the beginning of this 100 Days Program. If certain techniques or strategies worked for you in the past, they will usually work again. Even one small trick from an old program can help you overcome any current struggles with staying on your plan.

What worked before?

In the past, what did you do to stick with your diet program? How did you keep yourself on track, even through difficult days? Try to recall specific actions or techniques you used during times when you were successful. Have you stopped doing some of the things that previously kept you focused? If so, what got in your way or pulled you off track?

As you think back to times when you've done well, pull out the tiniest details that previously helped you stick with your efforts. Then use all of your old tricks to boost your current plan. Here are a few ideas:

- At my coffee break, I did deep breathing exercises to manage my stress.

- I went dancing every week. It always helped me work off my frustration.

- I worked out my anger by pulling weeds in my garden.

- I picked out great relaxing music and played it on my drive home from work.

- I took art classes instead of going out with my friends.

Pull out your old tricks

What about times when you managed your emotional needs without reaching for food? You probably used a lot of tricks to help you stay out of the refrigerator. Was anything in your life different at that time? Were you less stressed or not as angry? Perhaps you were in a different relationship or you had a better job, more friends, and lots of support.

Don't let your present circumstances keep you from making progress. Instead of getting stuck on what you can't do, figure out what things you can salvage from your past. Most of the mental images and self-talk phrases that helped before will probably work again.

Even if your life is different now, you can still draw from what worked for you before. Maybe you laid your exercise clothes out at night or kept a water bottle in the refrigerator so you could grab it easily before you started your walk. Remember what used to work, then pull your best strategies back off the shelf and put them into your program again.

TODAY

- Make a list of all the best weight-management "tricks" you remember from your past.

- Put a star beside all the ones you could use again.

- Pick one idea to put into action today, and then do it!

❧ DAY 98 ❧

New Year's resolution

Imagine what your life will be like after you've reached your weight-loss goals. To help you picture this accomplishment, mentally fast-forward to one year from now. Pretend your current plan was successful and that you've lost weight, built an exercise program, and maintained your new habits.

Today you'll be creating a *New Year's resolution* in advance. In this vision of the future, you are at your ideal weight. You also have a great lifestyle that helps you stay at your goal.

First, assume that at this time next year, you'll have reached all of your goals. Then in your notebook or on a separate piece of paper write: "The date is _____, and here is what I've accomplished."

On the blank line, write *today's* month and day, but fill in the year as being one year from now.

Pretend it's happened

Based on what you'd like to see happen during the next year, write an outcome for each of the areas below. Don't be afraid to dream big. Assume that you will look and feel the way you desire, and then write your list from that optimistic viewpoint.

- I now weigh _____ (write down the amount you want to weigh one year from now).

- I'm pleased with _____ (include your dream outcomes such as better energy, body changes, new attitude).

214

- My body feels _____ (use words like *strong, healthy, slender, thinner, toned*).

- I'm exercising by _____ (list your exercise activities as well as how often you're doing them).

- I've learned _____ (list items such as how to stop emotional eating, cope with stress, or build motivation).

You can make it happen

When you've completed all of the statements, read your New Year's resolution out loud. How do these words make you feel? Hopeful? Wonderful? Scared? You probably have all of these responses. And yet, the picture you've just created can come true.

Even though you still have work ahead of you, holding this future vision is critical to your success right now. When you have a clear image of your goals, it's easier to determine what you have to do to make them happen.

TODAY

- Complete the exercise listed above and record your New Year's resolution in your notebook.

- Make a collage or a drawing of your future. Look for magazine pictures such as people jogging and then use them to represent your goals. Add words such as *energized, strong, peaceful,* or *fun loving*.

- Use this picture of the future to help inspire you concerning your current actions.

❧ DAY 99 ❧
It's not in here!

No matter how long you stay on your diet or maintenance plan, food will still always look good! And you'll never be completely free of the temptation to eat something when you feel stressed or upset and need nurturing and solace.

On days when the world lets you down, food will always have an appeal. It's simply quick, easy, and available, giving you an instant solution to whatever's troubling you.

To safeguard yourself from struggles with emotional eating, you've learned many tricks, such as placing notes on your mirror or repeating certain phrases to yourself. But here's one more way to catch yourself before you dig into the food.

Before opening, read the sign

Make a sign that says, *"It's not in here!"* Then place it at eye level on your refrigerator or your cupboard. Whenever you start to open those doors, read the sign and remind yourself that food cannot be a solution to your emotional needs.

Then pull out all your resources for emotional coping and do something else. Instead of staring into the refrigerator at the end of the day, use healthier ways to get an "instant fix." Keep some baby carrots or celery available for when you want to chew on your boss. Maintain a good supply of your favorite teas or special diet sodas within easy reach.

Find the perfect music to play on those days when you're troubled or exhausted. Store the music in your CD player or other device so you can hit the "play" button as soon as you get in the car or walk through your front door.

Move toward joy

While eating can certainly give you pleasure, it doesn't bring real peace or joy. After a difficult day, food won't provide the true level of nurturing and satisfaction you seek. So instead of eating to feel better, look for a solution that will address your real needs.

Continue to discover what works for you, and then use these tricks again and again to help you manage life without reaching for food. If you weaken and you're tempted to rip open the cookies or chips, remind yourself: "What I really need isn't in here!" Then look for healthy ways to address your needs and move closer to the true joy of life.

TODAY

- Make a sign that says, "It's not in here!" Post it in an obvious place on your refrigerator. Write the same words in your notebook, and then define exactly what they mean to you.

- If your solution isn't found in the cupboard or the refrigerator, where will you find it?

- Create a list of instant resources you can use when you're sliding toward emotional eating.

✹ DAY 100 ✹

This is how I live!

One of the most common themes among dieters is the phrase, *"I know what to do, I just don't do it."* During the past 100 days, I hope you've come a long way from that one. But even with successful dieters, there's another problem that often occurs. As time goes by, eventually they will confess, *"I forgot what I know!"*

Right now you're feeling excited, motivated, and quite focused on maintaining your success. But with time, all of your tools will begin to slip from your conscious mind. Eventually you can forget even the most valuable ones—unless you develop a system for remembering them.

Your top 10

From time to time you need a way to remind yourself of the principles you live by. You've probably recorded many of your favorite tools in your notebook. Now you need to go one step further and figure out how to make all of these concepts a permanent part of your life.

Start by selecting your favorite principles from the 100 Days Program. Then choose the top 10 lessons that fit best for you—the ones you want to live by long-term.

Write these down and then plan how you'll keep them in mind forever. Think about what would help you remember your tools. Do you need to make an audio tape or CD so you can listen to your own advice while you're driving or cleaning? Maybe you could create a colorful poster for your bathroom wall or post a list of tools on the computer at your office.

Foundation for a lifetime

After you've chosen the guidelines you want to follow forever, you can use them as a foundation for your daily life. To make this easier, create a notebook page or a sign that proclaims, *"This is how I live!"*

Then list your top 10 skills along with any other principles or values that you want to keep in your life long-term. You might even revise your list once in a while, pulling in a few new concepts along with the old ones. Even though you won't always follow these perfectly, at least you'll remember your lifetime goals. Ten or twenty years from now, you should be able to pull out this same list and affirm it's still true.

Yes, this is how I live!

TODAY

- Decide what methods you'll use to remember your favorite tools from the 100 Days Program.

- In your notebook, make a "top 10 list" that includes all of the concepts you plan to use forever.

- Create a plan for how you will keep these ideas in front of you *always!*

219

DAYS 91–100 COMPLETED!

Congratulations!

You've made it through all 100 days.

Now it's time for you to become a long-term success!

You've finished the 100 Days of Weight Loss Program! But don't stop now! Think about what you need to do next. Would it help to repeat the 100 Days lessons to cement them more strongly into your life? Do you need to focus on your top 10 skills for a while until they become routine in your days?

Make sure you integrate all of the things you've learned into a daily lifetime plan that will help you maintain your weight. Then keep learning more and adding to your skills.

Always remember the words, "A decision about what to weigh is a decision about how to live." If you follow this principle and use your skills and tools every single day, long-term success is practically guaranteed!

❧ INDEX ❧